READY, SET, MEMOIR!

The Essential Guide to Telling Your Story

By Lindsey Grant of National Novel Writing Month

CHRONICLE BOOKS
SAN FRANCISCO

For Mira and Ben
Thank you for making the deadline challenging
but achievable.

ISBN 978-1-7972-0800-8

Manufactured in China.

Design and illustrations by Jon Glick.

10 9 8 7 6 5 4 3 2 1

Chronicle books and gifts are available at
special quantity discounts to corporations,
professional associations, literary programs,
and other organizations. For details and
discount information, please contact our
premiums department at corporatesales@
chroniclebooks.com or at 1-800-759-0190.

Chronicle Books LLC
680 Second Street
San Francisco, California 94107
www.chroniclebooks.com

CONTENTS

INTRODUCTION
6

CHAPTER 1:
WHAT IS A MEMOIR, ANYWAY?
8

CHAPTER 2:
MANAGING THE *I* IN MEMOIR
26

CHAPTER 3:
SCOPING YOUR STORY
40

CHAPTER 4:
MAXIMIZING *WHAT* AND *WHEN*
52

CHAPTER 5:
ORDERING THE EVENTS
64

CHAPTER 6:
FILLING IN THE BLANKS
78

CHAPTER 7:
REST, RESET, REVISE!
94

CHAPTER 8:
OVERCOMING THE INEVITABLE
107

CHAPTER 9:
THE RESOURCE ROOM
122

ACKNOWLEDGMENTS
136

ABOUT THE AUTHOR
136

Introduction

WELCOME TO YOUR WORKBOOK!

I'm delighted you want to write a memoir. You look ready. Whether you're here as a NaNoWriMo participant, or you have no idea what NaNoWriMo is, you've come to the right place for plenty of memoir-writing guidance, expert advice, encouragement, support, and a few coloring exercises, too.

For the uninitiated, NaNoWriMo stands for "National Novel Writing Month," a free, web-based nonprofit that encourages writers around the world to draft their novel—and now, memoir—in a month. It's enormously enjoyable, and you should check it out at Nanowrimo.org. I came to NaNoWriMo in 2004 as their volunteer coordinator; in 2008 I became program director. In 2011, Chris Baty (founder of NaNoWriMo), Tavia Stewart (employee #2), and I published *Ready, Set, Novel!*, a writer's workbook for NaNoWriMo participants—or anyone, really—to plan and plot the first draft of their novel. This follow-up provides the same fun yet effective approach for aspiring memoirists.

As you enter your workbook, please feel free to wipe your feet on this first page.

You can, if you choose, use this workbook in conjunction with NaNoWriMo's one-month drafting deadline—it's yours, so you're in charge. To help you decide what works best, here's a quick behind-the-scenes look at its structure:

Chapters 1–6 will help you plan your memoir. If you're new to the genre, or you'd like to start your month-long memoir challenge with an established idea of what you're writing, prepare to complete these activities before you start your first draft.

Chapter 7 is full of "after you draft" activities to help you refine and polish your manuscript before sharing it with others.

Chapter 8 is like your own personal Help Desk, staffed 24/7 with antidotes to common creative setbacks.

Chapter 9 is stocked with resources *and* refreshments; reading, media, author platform and memoir-development recommendations; and plenty of congratulations for your commendable efforts. Think of a literary salon, but with confetti.

Whichever way you choose to tackle these chapters, I am excited to go on this journey with you and help where and when I can. As part memoir–planning concierge, part agony aunt, I know we're going to get this thing done, and have a big party in the process.

LET'S GET STARTED!

CHAPTER 1

WHAT IS A MEMOIR, ANYWAY?

CHECKLIST

- [ ] Toolbox
- [ ] Food for Thought with Piper Kerman & Leigh Stein
- [ ] Solving the Memoir Mystery
- [ ] 'Gram It
- [ ] Finding Your Venn
- [ ] Memoirs You Know and Love
- [ ] Good News, Great News
- [ ] Rules of the Game

Congratulations are in order!

You took the first critical steps toward writing your memoir. You bought this book, cracked open the cover, and (presumably) read the introduction. Here you are on the cusp of Chapter 1! Huzzah! High five.

Still, you may be thinking, "What am I doing here?! I'm not a memoirist!" or "What even *is* a memoir?!" This chapter will help you answer both questions, and more.

Why you're here

You have a story to tell—a story about yourself, your experiences, and your life. You never would have started down this path if that weren't the case. Still, knowing there's a personal story you'd like to share doesn't mean you know how to share it—how to take the stuff of real life and make it engaging, relatable, and poignant for readers that aren't your mom or partner or whomever your biggest fan might be. Before we go one step further, I'd like you to please turn and face your doubt, lurking behind you with bad hair, bad breath, and heaps of misgivings, and say, "I have a story to tell!"

A little louder, please: "I HAVE A STORY TO TELL!"

Excellent. That, writer, is why you're here.

So, what is a memoir?

Memoir and autobiography, while both genres of nonfiction in which the author writes about themselves, are not interchangeable terms. That's not to say that there isn't some gray area within the genre, or that you can't get wildly creative with what you include in your memoir or how you include it. Together, we can look at what sets memoir distinctly apart from other forms of nonfiction, especially autobiography.

With this knowledge in hand, you will look at the key elements of some published memoirs before figuring out what will define your own.

What will your memoir be, and why?

By the end of this chapter, you'll know what your memoir is about, so you can start tackling the other story elements fundamental to a book-length narrative. You'll understand why, of all the stories you could tell, you're writing this one right now. You've already told your doubts to step off. Armed with the information you gain in this chapter, you'll be managing your main character—you—with courage and confidence. So, let's get going!

Toolbox

Before you begin this chapter, think about what memoirs you've read and remember. Maybe you're not sure if it is a memoir, but you know it is nonfiction. We can parse the genre together. If possible, gather a few examples—either digital books or hard copies—to reference as you go. List the titles you've selected here.

Michael J Fox   Lucky Man
Louis Theroux   Gotta Get Theroux
                 This
Adam Kay — All of them
Bob Mortimer
Michael Rosen
Jay Blades.

It never hurts to have a beverage and snack at hand, either, and some epic music to get your blood pumping and the ideas flowing. My go-tos these days are dried mango, endless coffee, and the *Gladiator* soundtrack (or anything by Hans Zimmer, really). I find that when I am dragging my feet, and my desk is more procrastination station than productivity pod, these things motivate me—incentives to get my butt in the seat and my fingers flying. Maybe your motivators are a favorite pair of sweats and a writing hat, or your co-author cat. (I have one of those, but his grammar is appalling.)

I think of these helpmates as a shield of sorts, fending off lethargy and distraction. At left is what mine looks like these days:

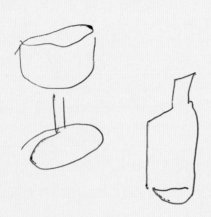

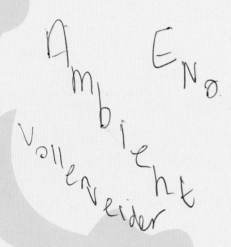

You can make a shield, too, bearing your own creative coat of arms.

Food for Thought

"On a dark and stormy night,"
"Once upon a time,"
"A long time ago and far, far away,"

Piper Kerman had this to say about her memoir, *Orange Is the New Black*:

"I was always really clear that what I wanted to write about was that sort of compressed and intense period of incarceration. In other words, I wasn't looking to write a book about my life in its entirety; I wasn't looking to write a book focused on the crime I'd committed 10 years prior to being incarcerated. What was interesting to me was the experience of incarceration for me as an individual, but—even more importantly—how my own experience as an individual fit into the bigger picture and how I was part of this community of women during the time that I was incarcerated."

Leigh Stein has described memoirs as

"a slice of your life—a dramatic slice of your life. A moment in your life that changed fundamentally your future; that divides your life into before and after."

Sit with that quote for a moment. When you're ready, tuck it into your toolbox. You'll want it for upcoming activities!

Solving the Memoir Mystery

In her interview on the Write-Minded podcast, Leigh Stein, author of *Land of Enchantment*, said, "I think there's a fundamental misunderstanding among people that aren't necessarily writers that [when] I say 'memoir,' I mean autobiography. So, a layperson, when I tell them I'm writing a memoir, would look at me and think, 'why does anyone care about your childhood up to your '30s?'"

If autobiography is an author's life story from beginning to the time of publication, how is a memoir different? The scope of memoir is limited to a portion of an author's life, defined by a specific subject, experience, or time frame. The author selectively includes stories, memories, insights, and experiences that tell a more focused story; by the same token, the author necessarily leaves out a great deal of personal history because it doesn't serve to inform or support the focus of the memoir. Thus, you, as a memoirist, must become something of a curator, mining the stuff of your life for those things that fit within the scope of the memoir and discarding that which is extraneous.

But we'll get to the mining later.

You grabbed a stack of nonfiction—presumably memoirs—for your toolbox. How did you know they were memoirs? (No fair if *A Memoir* is printed on the front cover of the book!) What clues do the book jacket, subtitle, or cover art offer to suggest that this is memoir and not autobiography? Make note of the clues you find.

_____

_____

_____

_____

_____

_____

_____

_____

_____

_____

_____

_____

If, in your investigation, you've determined that some of your selected titles are in fact autobiography, set them aside for the time being and focus on those titles you know are memoirs.

'Gram It

Building on Leigh Stein's suggestion that memoirs are a slice of the author's life with a discernible "before and after" moment that frames that story, this exercise will help us visualize the "slice of life" addressed in your favorite memoirs.

An early example of the genre is *12 Years a Slave*, by Solomon Northup. A free man living in New York, Northup was abducted and sold into slavery. This book details those twelve years of his life. Northup's memoir doesn't cover every aspect of his life from birth; neither is it a comprehensive accounting of slavery in the US, or even New Orleans, where he was enslaved. Instead, Northup's memoir is an intersection of all these subjects. He details his own experience and observations of slavery in New Orleans, sharing myriad personal experiences from his twelve years of enslavement while also educating the reader on such topics as cotton farming and sugar production, and the unique geography and climate of New Orleans.

It's helpful for me to think of a memoir's scope like a Venn diagram, where the author's life story and the specific subject matter or experience overlap. In this way, the memoir is the intersection of the author's experience of the subject matter, complete with background details pulled from the author's life, as well as contextual information about the specific topic, time frame, or experience.

Solomon Northup's
life story

12 Years a Slave

Enslavement in
New Orleans

For those titles you've been studying—or maybe some new titles you're now remembering—see which you can identify as a memoir using the blank Venn diagrams.

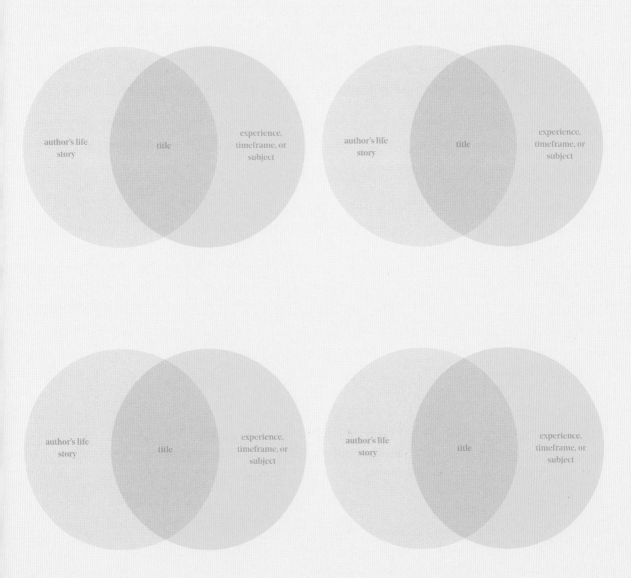

Finding Your Venn

Let's turn our attention now to how your story fits into this memoir framework. What slice of life will you focus on? What is your before and after moment? If you're not sure, or you have several in mind, start by writing them all down here.

The life of Symo
My life in Disability Arts
Working with people with learning Disability

If you're not ready to commit yet, or you're not sure which idea would make the best memoir, feel free to sit with this for a little while. You may even end up refining your choice or changing your mind entirely! In the meantime, ask yourself these questions to see if it helps the decision-making process:

Which of these experiences or moments in your life are you most excited to write about?

Symo

Asked differently, which of these ideas feels the most urgent to you, and why?

SYmo becuse I'm 61 and have the most recollection

Which of these do you have the most to say (and thus, write) about?

Dis Arts

When you're ready, fill in your Venn. If you're still unsure, feel free to use Post-its, a pencil, or an erasable pen.

If it's helpful to you, post a copy of this diagram near your computer screen or any other prominent place in your writing space.

Memoirs You Know and Love

Just like any writer—or any artist, for that matter—memoirists have distinctive writing styles that make their work unique. Some rely heavily on dialogue and scenes, while others are more into exposition. Some are quite poetic, while others are defined by humorous observations. Think, for example, of essayist David Sedaris (author of *Me Talk Pretty One Day* and *Dress Your Family in Corduroy and Denim*, among many others) as compared to Norman Maclean (who wrote *A River Runs Through It*). Both write powerfully of their families, childhoods, and formative experiences and memories, yet their authorial voices couldn't be more different.

A couple of pages ago, you wrote down the titles of a few memoirs you've read and remember. Take some time to unpack the stylistic decisions of each, considering, too, what you enjoy about each. Is the writing wordy or spare? Are the writer's observations often humorous or more poignant? How much dialogue is included? How is the book structured? And importantly, what is the book about? Is it just a story of the writer's life, or is there an overarching theme or timeframe the writer focuses on that frames the work?

Title(s)

_____

_____

_____

Stylistic elements

_____

_____

_____

_____

_____

_____

_____

_____

_____

_____

What I like about this book

_____
_____
_____
_____
_____
_____
_____
_____
_____
_____
_____
_____
_____
_____
_____
_____
_____
_____
_____
_____

What this book is about

_____
_____
_____
_____
_____
_____
_____
_____
_____
_____
_____
_____
_____
_____
_____
_____
_____
_____
_____

Good News, Great News

Now that you have an idea of what your memoir will be about, you'll have a ready answer when people ask you, "Hey, what's your memoir about?" You also have an idea of what you want your memoir to be like, stylistically speaking, and what devices you can use or include to make your memoir distinctively yours. This is good news. Really good news. But it gets even better.

The great news is that the shape of your memoir—its narrative arc—can be as familiar as you want it to be. Stories, whether fiction or nonfiction, have many of the same elements. Whether you've already tried your hand at writing fiction, or you've read pretty much any book ever, you'll be familiar with the ingredients that make up a story.

This is not to say all stories utilize all these elements, or in equal amounts. There are so many wonderful memoirs that blend genres, break rules, and establish all new ways of relating personal stories. You may find that once you understand the basics of memoir, you're interested in defying the conventions.

As a first-time memoirist, you may wish to adhere to a more familiar format, utilizing the time-tested building blocks of narrative to create your true-life tale. Let's look at these building blocks together:

Plot: You're well on your way when it comes to plot, having established the components of your memoir in previous exercises. In later chapters and activities, your plot will become more detailed as you integrate other essential elements of the story. For now, though, try summarizing your memoir's plot. You can even include aspects of the style you've chosen. For example, my memoir's summary might be "A tragicomic recounting of my time as a dog walker and pet sitter in the San Francisco Bay Area after I graduated from college." If it's helpful, try a couple different versions to see what works best for you!

Characters: Virtually every story has a character or characters, be they human, animal, inanimate, or imaginary. While memoirs are unique in that the primary character is also the author, even real-life characters, both primary and supporting, have the same emotional makeup as fictional ones. Any character has needs, wants, fears, strengths, and flaws. As you craft your memoir, you'll highlight those same aspects that make any character—real or imagined—dimensional, believable, and someone your care for enough to read a book about them. Everyone in your life won't feature in your memoir, just as you won't include every experience you've ever had. You will, however, determine in later exercises which people factor prominently enough in this specific story you're telling to be included as characters. And you'll want them to feel as real, rich, and relatable on the page as they are in real life. Look at your stack of nonfiction and memoirs gathered for the toolbox on page 10. Who, other than the author, is featured as a character? And how are these characters drawn? What makes them effectively written? Is there a person (or maybe it's a thing!) that stands in the way of your main character's (ahem . . . *your*) success? That will be your antagonist—an important person (or thing) that will contribute to a dramatic story arc.

Character arc: This one is pretty straightforward, but maybe not something you even realize is happening in a story unless you look for it. How do the main and/or supporting characters, and even the antagonist, change throughout the course of the story? Be it a book or a movie, fiction or documentary, any story would be pretty boring—and actually depressing—if its characters stayed exactly the same in the face of everything that happens from the first page to the last. Consider your sample stack of nonfiction, or any other story that comes immediately to mind, and how the characters exhibit changes from beginning to end. What did each want more than anything? And what did they sacrifice—or what were they unwilling to sacrifice—to get what they wanted or needed? Who has a change of heart, and why?

_____

_____

_____

_____

_____

_____

Setting: An oft-overlooked part of many stories, the setting can be as important to a story as the characters that populate it. A powerful sense of place grounds a story in reality, which is crucial for memoirs. Making sure your readers can feel the essence of the place or places in your memoir—its history, local culture, the people, weather, architecture, and energy—will go a long way toward keeping your reader captivated by and invested in the story you're telling. Return to the stories you know, and especially those nonfictional ones, and how setting factored into the work. How was the place depicted? Was there more than one setting? Were they equally detailed in their descriptions? What worked well? What did you wish you knew more about?

_____

_____

_____

_____

_____

_____

_____

_____

Subplot: The richest stories aren't only about one thing. "Wait," you may be thinking. "We already established that my memoir is about me *and* [insert subject of your memoir here]." That's true. Memoir is an intersection of two main components. But simultaneous to the main subject matter is often a secondary story, unfolding apace with the primary action. I know—it sounds like a lot, and not all stories have it or need it. However, it *is* a worthwhile thing to consider as you look at those sample titles you gathered for your toolbox at the beginning of the chapter. Is there a secondary plotline in any of them, and if so, what is it? In my memoir *Sleeps with Dogs*, I primarily write about walking dogs and housesitting. I also address the stuff of establishing myself as a functioning adult far from home—paying bills, keeping my car running, a roof over my head, and, ultimately, finding love. That secondary storyline runs parallel to my adventures in animal nannying, occasionally intersecting at crucial moments to reinforce the progression of the plot or the character's growth. Thinking of some stories you know and love, what great subplots come to mind? How about in your favorite nonfiction? Use the provided space to make note of any memoir subplots you identify—or, perhaps, ideas you have for your own!

Rules of the Game

Whether you pursue a more traditional narrative, relying upon the building blocks of story creation we've covered here, or you choose to color outside the lines with your memoir, there are a few important guidelines to writing a memoir that we should address early and will reinforce often.

It must be true. Ah, truth. It's subjective, it's slippery, and it's debatable. When it comes to truth in memoir, I am talking about *your* truth. How it happened to *you*; what it meant for *you*; how *you* experienced an event, an individual's actions, or an aspect of your life. Undoubtedly, people remember, feel, and understand things very differently. Each of us is entitled to our own version of the truth. Your mandate is to adhere to your personal truth, and not skew it or betray it for dramatic impact or narrative convenience. Readers have reliable bullhonky detectors: Breaking their trust is a grave offense. You also have an internal truth-o-meter, and you'll know when you're veering away from truth-telling and into the realm of tall tales. Remembering things exactly as they happened can be hard, especially when re-creating dialogue. We will address these sticky wickets in later chapters and activities to help you figure out how to keep honesty and authenticity front and center in your memoir.

It must have happened to you. No fair co-opting other people's experiences as your own. You may absolutely depict an event or experience that you witnessed or were privy to, focusing on how it impacted or changed you. But don't blur the lines of ownership. As I said before, you and your reader both know if you're playing fast and loose with the facts, so cleave to reality. If you're imagining an alternative history, tell your reader that's what you're doing.

Even if it is true and it happened to you and it's funny or interesting or dramatic, it still may not belong in your memoir. Did you post the Venn diagram of your memoir's plot somewhere in your workspace? If not, turn back to page 17. That intersection of your life and your subject matter, that's what your memoir is about. If the anecdote, moment, or scene you wish to include doesn't fall within the clearly defined boundaries of your memoir, driving this specific story's development or providing relevant backstory, it probably doesn't belong.

Even if it's true, it happened to you, and it fits within the defined scope of your memoir, always question your motives. A general rule of thumb is that you shouldn't ever include something to make you look good or make someone else look bad. That doesn't mean you need to throw it out completely, but effective writing usually doesn't come with an agenda. Your reader will appreciate the nuance of the moment if you're willing to be vulnerable in your self-assessments and generous in your assessment of others.

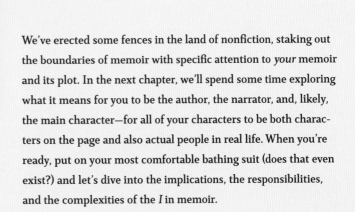

Coming Up

We've erected some fences in the land of nonfiction, staking out the boundaries of memoir with specific attention to *your* memoir and its plot. In the next chapter, we'll spend some time exploring what it means for you to be the author, the narrator, and, likely, the main character—for all of your characters to be both characters on the page and also actual people in real life. When you're ready, put on your most comfortable bathing suit (does that even exist?) and let's dive into the implications, the responsibilities, and the complexities of the *I* in memoir.

CHAPTER 2

THE *I* IN MEMOIR

CHECKLIST

- [ ] Food for Thought with Jill Swenson
- [ ] Facing (and Banishing) Your Fears
- [ ] Donning the Character Cape
- [ ] Characterization Station
- [ ] Meeting Your Main Character
- [ ] Villain Shoes
- [ ] The Stuff of Legends

On her website, Swenson Book Development, Jill Swenson deftly sums up your unique role as a memoirist. "A memoir requires a writer collapse three roles into one: author, narrator, and protagonist." You are always wearing three hats, which is a lot to manage!

In the previous chapter we addressed some ways that you maintain your integrity as an author: tell the truth, and tell *your* truth, not anyone else's. As far as your responsibilities as a narrator go, we also highlighted the importance of motivation when it comes to what stories you tell about yourself and others. *Why* are you including these stories about yourself or others? Hopefully, every detail/memory/moment supports the scope of the story and isn't there to make you seem great and your enemies seem gross. (More on that soon.)

Because you are your memoir's main character, or protagonist, the reader is most connected to you as a character and your progress, successes, setbacks, and challenges throughout the course of the memoir.

In this chapter, you'll work on identifying those aspects of character—needs and wants, adversaries and obstacles—for the protagonist (who, yes, happens to be you) and the other characters in your book. The idea is to create enough distance between you and that main character on the page that you can write about yourself and others—including anyone or anything standing in your path to glory or trying to trip you up—honestly and with the depth necessary to draw effective, believable characters that serve your story while still remaining true to life.

Food for Thought

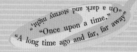

"If your public persona as an author doesn't match with the character description and narrative voice in your memoir, readers will find you disingenuous and inauthentic. You shall be judged by readers in three ways. As an author. As a narrator. As a protagonist."

–Jill Swenson

Did you just read the phrase, "You shall be judged by readers. . . " and freeze up? Freak out? Please proceed with haste to the next section so we can tackle this anxiety together.

Facing (and Banishing) Your Fears

Yeah, I get it. It's not enjoyable to be on the receiving end of judgment. Especially if, as the quote suggests, it rains down upon you in three fun flavors. Writing about yourself, your fears, your flaws, and your vulnerabilities is scary. Writing about other people in your life is scary. Digging up memories and rehashing old conversations and experiences can also be scary. Very scary! But if you flip back to page 9 where we establish why you're here, you'll recall that you have a story to tell. Yes, it happens to be a story about you, and features people you know, many of whom you care about immensely and whose opinions matters a great deal to you. None of this changes the fact that you have a story you feel strongly about sharing.

When I set out to write my own memoir, I was also writing a story I urgently needed to tell, but I was still paralyzed by fear—of offending people, of being accused of slander, of sharing my worst qualities with the world, of getting things wrong. So afraid was I that my first draft was written in the third person and passed off as fiction. And you know what? It stunk—of inauthenticity and affectation and old bananas. It was totally inauthentic and affected, though I can't explain the banana smell.

By the time my memoir was published, countless drafts and almost eight years later, I was still nervous about people's reactions, but I also knew I didn't need to worry about authenticity or honesty because I had embraced my truth and I could stand by every word. And you know what happened? Not a single person objected. Not one! No offense taken, and no lawsuits. By making myself vulnerable and sharing the good, the bad, and the malodorous, I also did the necessary work of making myself relatable to the reader.

Dear writer, please believe that if you tell your truth, if you don't try to cast yourself as falsely heroic and instead portray yourself as a person, warts and all, you'll be writing about someone the reader can understand and root for. At the same time, if you are generous and sympathetic in your rendering of other people in your memoir—especially those you've crossed swords with—readers will be able to understand them and their motivations, too.

Be honest, be generous, and instead of fearing your readers' judgment, trust it. Believe that if you are open and honest, readers will judge you and your story fairly. I think you'll find that when you write without fear, you have nothing to fear. Only if you write fearfully, evasively, or manipulatively will you have reason to dread the readers' response.

Donning the Character Cape

One way I was able to tamp down my anxiety over writing about myself and other real-life people was to think of "us"—all the real-life people portrayed in my memoir—as characters. There had to be enough distance between "me" and the me I was writing about so that I could see myself with some objectivity. I had to split myself into writer "me" and character "me."

This goes for anyone else I included in those pages. I needed a mental barrier that allowed me to write, for example, about my now-husband/then-boyfriend, how we met, and what our early relationship was like without worrying about or overthinking his reaction to my recollections and anecdotes.

Like Clark Kent and his glasses—or any superhero's mantle, for that matter—I had to don a disguise that allowed for this duality. It made me both more productive and significantly less sweaty.

Take a moment to fashion your own version of a superhero's disguise. Is it a mask? Fancy underpants? Fingerless gloves? Whatever it is, it should allow you to write about yourself—and anyone else in your story—with honesty, generosity, and an utter lack of anxiety-induced perspiration.

To get on with the necessary and brave work of memoir-writing, draw your own disguise in the wardrobe.

Characterization Station

As we discussed in Chapter 1, one of the most effective ways to figure out how to do something is to see how someone else does it. (Think about all those YouTube videos you've watched recently: making bowtie pasta, folding a napkin into a swan, latte art. Am I right?)

In the spirit of watching and learning, let's look at how your favorite (or any) memoirist has written about himself or herself. You'll find, I wager, that the author's self-portrait bears all the hallmarks of a fully realized character.

What was their greatest need or want?

_____
_____
_____

Greatest fear?

_____
_____
_____
_____
_____

What were they willing to do (or not do!) to get what they wanted or needed?

_____
_____
_____
_____

Did they have any flaws or weaknesses?

_____
_____
_____
_____
_____

Is there something standing in the way of the main character getting where they need to go or what they need more than anything else in the world (keeping in mind that sometimes this obstacle is human but sometimes it is an illness, or poverty, or something even more intangible like self-doubt).

_____
_____
_____
_____

Has the main character changed by the end of the book? How?

_____
_____
_____
_____

What makes the character especially likeable or relatable? Or, if the character isn't such a great person, what redeems them? Why do you care enough to read a book about this person?

_____
_____
_____
_____
_____

And, perhaps most importantly, were there things the author wrote about himself or herself that did not ring true for you? Why did you feel this way?

_____
_____
_____
_____
_____
_____
_____

Meeting Your Main Character

You've looked at how another author wrote themself as the main character of a memoir. Now it's time to consider your own memoir and yourself as that main character, shortened here to "MC." Answer the same questions as they pertain to the hero of your story.

What is your MC's greatest need or want?

_____
_____
_____
_____
_____
_____
_____
_____

Greatest fear?

_____
_____
_____
_____
_____
_____
_____
_____

What is the MC willing to do (or not do!) to get what they want or need most?

_____
_____
_____
_____
_____
_____
_____

Does the MC have any flaws or weaknesses?

_____

_____

_____

_____

_____

Is there a villain in this story? Who (or what) is preventing the main character from achieving their goal?

_____

_____

_____

_____

_____

_____

Has the main character changed by the end of the book? How?

_____

_____

_____

_____

_____

_____

_____

_____

_____

_____

_____

_____

_____

_____

_____

_____

_____

Villain Shoes

We have already highlighted what flaws, needs, wants, and fears that you, the main character, have. You also identified what stands in the way of your main character getting their happily ever after. This obstacle to happiness, fulfillment, success, or wellness is the antagonist, or villain, and requires just as much dimensionality, nuance, and relatability as the main character.

Now, this obstacle/antagonist/villain may not necessarily be a person. Looking at the stack of memoirs in your toolbox, take a moment to identify the maleficent obstacle thwarting the main character in one or a few of these books.

_____

_____

_____

_____

_____

_____

_____

_____

_____

_____

_____

_____

_____

_____

_____

_____

_____

_____

_____

_____

How many of these so-called villains were human beings? Some? None?

Looking to your own memoir and the notes you made in the previous exercise, take a moment to reflect on the treacherous obstacle to your own main character's happiness. Even if the antagonist isn't human, let's imagine this villain's got some villainous shoes, and you need to put them on to fully flesh out the ways in which its needs are at odds with the main character's.

Go ahead, don those smelly villain kicks. Other than thwarting the success of your main character, what does your antagonist need or want to survive—or achieve total world domination—and why? (You can apply this concept to anything—not just humans. What would a fascist regime need to thrive? Or a disease?)

How does the success of the villain undermine the success of the main character?

_____

_____

_____

_____

_____

_____

_____

_____

_____

_____

What, if anything, can you relate to about the villainous person, establishment, disease, or concept? What are their strengths or talents? (If your villain is a thing and not a person, one way to add dimensionality to its existence is to contemplate how maybe this thing, while bad for your main character, is good for other people or could be seen as positive in some lights.)

_____

_____

_____

_____

_____

_____

_____

_____

_____

_____

No matter what (or who) the villain in your memoir is, a fully realized antagonist with pros and cons, strengths and weaknesses, needs and wants, or dreams and fears of their own will enrich your memoir immeasurably and make your main character's plight so much more urgent in the process.

The Stuff of Legends

I have an important question for you: What makes *you*, the triple-hat wearing author/narrator/protagonist, a reliable narrator—neé, an authority—on this subject? Think of all the stories in your book about you and the subject of your memoir. What is the first impression you want to give your reader about your relationship to the topic?

In the first pages of *Sleeps with Dogs*, I share two stories from childhood about being bitten by animals I was taking care of: our second-grade class hamster and a neighbor's Cocker Spaniel. I learned at an early age that animals bite when they're afraid. What I wanted more than anything was for animals to feel safe with me—yes, so I wouldn't get bitten, because that hurts, but also because it made me sad to think of the animal being frightened by me. I wanted them to feel comforted by me, not fearful or under attack. By leading with these particular stories, I was attempting to convey a lot of foundational information—that I have always loved animals, that I took their comfort and safety very seriously, and that even though I have always cared a lot about seeming friendly and gentle, I don't always get it quite right. I certainly didn't lead with stories about me being some kind of animal whisperer or entrepreneurial whiz at an early age. That wasn't true, and it also wouldn't fit the mood of memoir I was writing, which is chock full of misunderstandings, misadventures, and plenty of self-deprecating humor.

Fearlessly now (clutch that cape or mask close!), try your hand at writing a scene or two that illustrates your relationship to the subject of your memoir. Try to rely upon the principle of show versus tell, wherein you're letting a scene about something that you did or that happened to you do the work of sharing some important information about yourself with your reader. Don't tell them what to think about you; demonstrate some aspects about yourself through action so that they may draw their own conclusions about you as the main character of this story, and why they might want to take this journey with you through the subject matter you've chosen as the focus of your memoir.

Hear ye, hear ye! With these words, our intrepid writer has officially embarked upon this surprise-filled, challenge-strewn, and highly rewarding memoir-writing journey. I doff my cap to you, scribe. Write on!

CHAPTER 3:

SCOPING
YOUR STORY

CHECKLIST

- [ ] Food for Thought with Daisy Hernandez
- [ ] Raiding the Pantry of Your Mind
- [ ] Assembling the Ingredients
- [ ] Story Soup: Practice Round
- [ ] 'Gramming It Again
- [ ] What's in a Scene?

Back in Chapter 1, we established that memoir is about a certain period, experience, or theme in your life, and not your entire life to date. (That would be an autobiography.) Memoir is limited in scope by a key theme, period of time, or series of related experiences in your life. Using that framework, you created a diagram for your own memoir's focus. Copy it again here as a reference for the exercises in this chapter.

In Chapter 2, you started to think more about the characters that will be included in this story. Naturally, your main character—you—is in there, along with a roster of supporting characters that likely includes your antagonist, or villain (if the primary obstacle to the main character's success takes human form).

Now it's time to start thinking about everything that will be included in your memoir: which major and minor life events will make the cut, which memories provide backstory and context for the story you're telling, and which subtopics you'll need to flesh out to move your story forward. Details of setting feature here, as would historical events that happened within the memoir's timeframe or that come to bear on the memoir's subject matter.

There's a tension to this chapter, as you want to be sure to cast the net wide enough that you're capturing a diverse and representative and plentiful enough collection of experiences and observations to make a rich and rewarding memoir, but not so much as to dilute its essential core. Everything you include must support the subject you've selected; at the same time, you must curate enough content to write a book-length narrative.

Once you've winnowed and organized your narrative fodder, you can start thinking about what scenes from your life will serve to inform the reader and illustrate your story.

By the end of this section, you'll have established both the broad and fine strokes of your memoir's contents. Nothing here is permanent, though. You may find yourself returning again and again to the exercises in this chapter to adjust and refine the scope of your story as it changes and evolves, or as new revelations unfold throughout the writing process. Just as writing and story craft require some measure of order and discipline, they also demand flexibility, improvisation, and a willingness to adapt. Like a chef assembling your *mise en place*, you'll finish this chapter with a range of necessary ingredients prepped and ready for your use. You can use these to make a focused, carefully crafted memoir, but you may also find yourself reaching deep into the pantry for a deeply buried but crucial ingredient. Sharpen your knives, wash your hands, and tighten your apron. We're making a memoir today!

Food for Thought

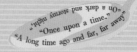

"On a dark and stormy night."
"Once upon a time."
"A long time ago and far, far away."

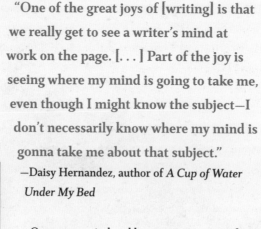

"One of the great joys of [writing] is that we really get to see a writer's mind at work on the page. [. . .] Part of the joy is seeing where my mind is going to take me, even though I might know the subject—I don't necessarily know where my mind is gonna take me about that subject."
—Daisy Hernandez, author of *A Cup of Water Under My Bed*

Open your mind and let association reign free for the first part of this chapter! You may be surprised to find all the places your mind takes you as you assess all the possibilities for what to include in your memoir.

Raiding the Pantry of Your Mind

Start listing everything you've been wanting to write about your life. At this stage, go wild—don't second guess yourself. You're free to throw anything in there that you think you might want in your book. You'd be surprised how many memories, moments, and anecdotes end up relating to and informing the focus of your memoir! Toss it all into the colander. We will rinse, reflect upon, and assess each ingredient before we decide whether it goes into the pot.

_____

_____

_____

_____

_____

_____

_____

_____

_____

_____

_____

_____

_____

_____

_____

_____

_____

_____

_____

Because memoirs are defined by a specific subject and how it uniquely intersects with your life, what you *don't* include becomes just as important as what you *do*. You may have found as you filled up your colander that you were identifying too broad a range of possible subjects and life moments—some of which are major, some more minor—and they won't all end up in the book. Conversely, maybe you don't feel like you have enough. Don't worry, though. You can always come back and add more as ideas come to you. So how do you sort through all the possible memoir ingredients to determine what stays or goes, or how much of each subject to include? Turn the page to find out.

Assembling the Ingredients

One way of organizing all of these ideas that may or may not survive the "subject sieve" is by charting your subjects and how they relate to the pillars of your memoir—your life story and the specific subject matter you're writing about. This will help you map which stories and memories relate to you, the main character and narrator, or the subject of your memoir, or both, as well as how all the themes relate to one another.

In *12 Years a Slave*, for example, the range of subjects Northup covers in his memoir might look something like this:

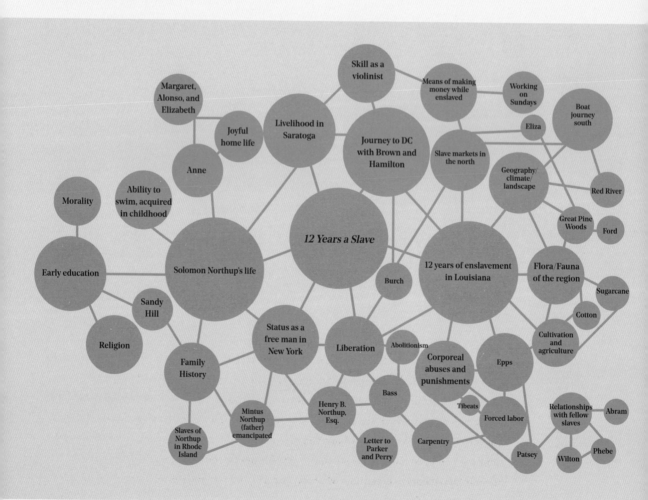

The level of detail could go on and on, with the bubbles getting ever smaller and more specific. Northup writes, for example, of Epps's son and his behaviors, mannerisms, and the casual cruelty that mirrors that of his father, even at ten or twelve years old. Northup's observations of the boy reinforce his belief that "with such training, whatever may be his natural disposition, it cannot well be otherwise that, on arriving at maturity, the sufferings and miseries of the slave will be looked upon with entire indifference." That alone could be a bubble, indicating a scene, reflection, or memory that comes to bear on the larger story. Or take, for example, the color red and its significance to enslaved women at Christmastime, which itself is a noteworthy component of Northup's narrative. The details, anecdotes, memories, and stories Northup chose to include in the memoir illustrate and inform the larger themes of the book, scene by scene. In some instances, Northup is present in the narrative only as the observer; the stories aren't only about his life but the lives of those people he interacted with, lived alongside, or whose abuses irrevocably changed the course of his life. Nevertheless, all these narrative threads comprise the greater story of Northup's understanding and experience of the institution of slavery.

Northup's enslavement occurred in adulthood, so those twelve years in which the narrative primarily occurs is his recent past. The rest of his life, when referenced, is recalled from his childhood or, to put it terms of Leigh Stein's "slice of life" paradigm—the "before." There are plenty of memoirs that largely take place in the distant past of the writer's childhood, youth, or early adulthood, such that the writer's more recent past—the "after"—features less in the story and its events are more carefully curated for inclusion in the memoir.

The balance between the left and right sides of this scoping diagram—those aspects of the author's life versus the specific subject matter of the memoir—may not always be balanced. Every memoir is unique; some have extensive flashbacks and frequently contextualize more recent events with backstory. Others focus more on exploring the subject matter at hand, not just as it relates to them and their past, but instead, for example, within a historical or cultural context. Later in the chapter, as you're organizing your own story, don't feel like there's a right or wrong way. This is simply a means of helping you visualize the topics you'll address in your memoir, how they relate to your life story, the specific experience or subject you're writing about, and how all the included information ties together.

Story Soup: Practice Round

Before you try your hand at ordering your story soup ingredients, practice by using a memoir you know well.

Using small Post-its or pencil (or go for it with ink! You're a star!), expand on the chart, creating variously sized bubbles with subjects and scenes, characters, and details both big and small. The provided bubbles are for, on the left, the author and narrator of the book; on the right, the unique subject matter that makes the memoir a memoir; and in the middle, your memoir's title. As you add bubbles, major themes get greater emphasis and thus will be bigger; supporting topics will be accordingly smaller.

It may take a number of attempts and lots of rearranging, and there are no right or wrong answers. In fact, a few variations will help you see how different emphasis changes the shape and tone of the book.

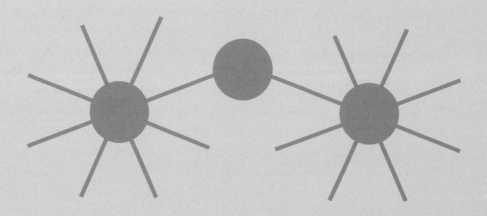

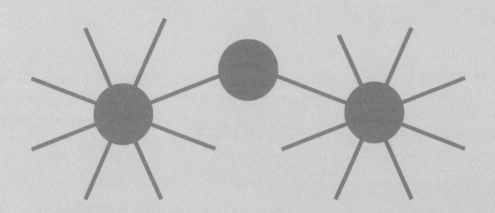

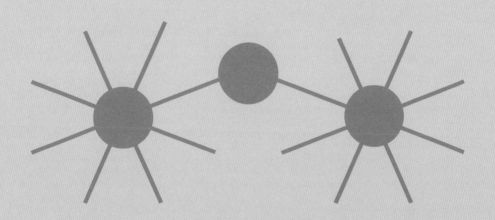

'Gramming It Again

No matter what kind of memoir soup you are cooking up, be it minestrone or mulligatawny, you're ready to start compiling all the story ingredients, seeing how they fit together and in what amounts. You already worked out the scope of someone else's memoir; now do the same for yours. Remember, you can use tiny Post-its or a pencil if you prefer. Be as specific or as broad at this stage as you like! You can always come back and add more detail as your understanding of your memoir grows and the scope becomes clearer to you.

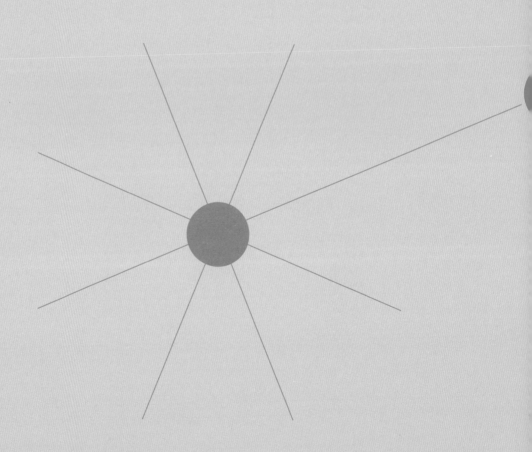

Once you've diagrammed your story, look back at your brainstorm on page 43, and that lengthy list of potential story ingredients you were putting through the story sieve. What didn't make it into the diagram, and why? Is there anything you left out that might belong? Or, conversely, is there anything you've added but doesn't really fit? After considering these offcuts and leftovers and their respective fates, sweep the remainders into the bin and call it good. You're scoping like a pro!

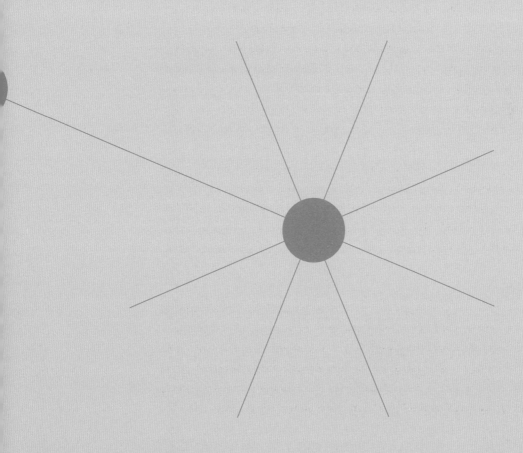

What's in a Scene?

In Chapter 1, you listed stylistic aspects you admire in published memoir. Take a moment to return to page 18 and refresh your memory.

Then, in Chapter 2, we talked a little bit about show versus tell, and you tried your hand at writing a scene that showcases your relationship to the subject matter of your memoir.

Looking now at a your collection of topics, memories, and anecdotes that fit within the scope of your story, start thinking about how you might put all of these pieces—content- *and* style-wise—together to craft the scenes that make up your memoir.

In addition to what you're writing about and how you write it, consider the following:

Dialogue can be tricky in memoir. Naturally, no one can remember the exact words that were spoken in every conversation, but you can certainly capture the meaning and tenor of key exchanges. However, dialogue is important to include to keep the story moving, to capture characters' personalities through speech patterns, and to keep the writing from getting bogged down in description. Trying to write a book-length work describing what people said without using any dialogue would quickly exhaust your reader and likely you, too. If you really can't remember the general thrust of a conversation, don't include it. Only focus on re-creating those vital exchanges that stick in your mind and had an impact on the subject matter at hand.

Avoid writing out "I remember. . ." as this is a given in memoir. Presumably, you remember all of it, otherwise it wouldn't be in your memoir, so there's no need to reiterate that fact. If at times you're trying to highlight the unreliability of your memory or how it differs from someone else's recollection, it's certainly okay to make an exception. However, as a general rule, the reader will know that flashbacks and reminiscences are based upon your memories of these events.

As much as possible, use action to illustrate character traits and development. Don't tell the reader how you, or anyone in your memoir, felt or changed—use your arsenal of memories and lived experience to craft scenes that do that work for you. Keeping the narrative active and full of movement will keep your reader engaged and the story moving far more effectively than if you adhere to a "Then this happened, then this happened, and I felt this way, and it made me think of this thing" approach to your recollections and recounting of life events.

If you're ready and willing, take everything you've learned thus far to write a scene or two.

_____

_____

_____

_____

_____

_____

_____

_____

_____

_____

_____

Were you able to write some dialogue? Was it difficult for you? The more you write dialogue, the easier it will come to you. In the meantime, it can be helpful to reflect on what initially feels hard or unnatural about it.

Looking back at what you wrote, what do you think each scene says? Does it show something larger about the time, place, or characters? Remember, just because it happened to you doesn't necessarily make it interesting to others. By the same token, just because it's interesting or important to you doesn't mean it's relevant to your memoir.

High-five here

Up High, Writer!

You've made huge progress in this chapter. Rest your pen or pencil so we can celebrate your efforts with some much-deserved high-fiving. Make that a high ten! (Double high fives? What is this called?) Bring it up high, writer!

Come on back to this page any time you need an extra dose of encouragement, ya hear?

CHAPTER 4

MAXIMIZING WHAT AND WHEN

CHECKLIST

- ☐ Food for Thought with Andrea J. Buchanan
- ☐ One Story, Three Ways
- ☐ What You Know/When You Know It
- ☐ The "What If" Game
- ☐ The Big Question(s)
- ☐ Legendary Moments, Revisited

In Chapter 3, we addressed what you want to include in your memoir, sourcing content from your own life while also considering what other background information or context the reader will need to understand your story and its subject matter. And before that, in Chapter 2, we took a moment to acknowledge our writerly fear of readers' judgments.

Here in Chapter 4, we've come to a funny paradox. On the one hand, we writers can't be drafting our stories with the specter of future readers hovering over our shoulders. On the other hand, there's a way in which we must write with the knowledge that we're crafting a narrative for other people's eyes. That audience will have readerly needs, wants, and yes, reactions. It seems like a contradiction to simultaneously banish the thought of future readers while also accommodating them. The trick here is to ignore any perceived judgments from future readers and instead focus on the ways you as the writer consider the essential "story needs" of the reader.

Now, it's true that you can't completely control your readers' responses to your story. Every individual that picks up your memoir will bring their own preconceived notions, experiences, and judgments, all of which influence their reaction to what you write. What you *can* control is when your readers learn certain details, and how you cast this information. As the writer, you hold the power to begin your memoir at any point and jump through space and time as you see fit. The way (and order!) in which you tell your story will absolutely affect your memoir's resonance with, and meaning to, readers.

In this chapter we will consider the effect of the information you dole out, so that you can make the most considered choices about when you share portions of your story and why. After all, any story—whether fiction or nonfiction—needs to sustain a reader's interest, earn their investment in the characters and outcomes, and meet the reader roughly halfway between what the writer explains and what the reader understands.

No memoirist sets out to write a boring, confusing, or frustrating narrative, though some might accidentally do it anyway. Once you complete this chapter, you'll be virtually immune to these pitfalls. Armed with a deeper understanding of how *what* and *when* factor into narrative structure, you can spend the next chapter ordering the events of your story for maximal effect.

Food for Thought

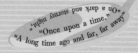

"On a dark and stormy night."
"Once upon a time."
"A long time ago and far, far away."

"We need stories to understand what's happening to us, and yet also there are limits to storytelling—how futile it can feel sometimes to come up with a story to explain the inexplicable! But I think that questioning process and that hopelessness of questioning the story is really crucial to finding where your version of the story lands."
—Andrea J. Buchanan, author of *Mother Shock: Loving Every (Other) Minute of It* and *The Beginning of Everything: The Year I Lost My Mind and Found Myself*

With Andi as our muse, let's challenge the seeming futility of storytelling by questioning how we choose to tell our stories and why. This way, we will mastermind what goes where for a maximally effective memoir.

One Story, Three Ways

Imagine a story about a train crash. You, the reader, find out in the first pages who was on the train, who was injured, who died, and what caused the crash. The rest of the story is spent leading up to this catastrophic event, building layers of tension and dispensing new information about the people and the crash that changes how you might feel about the event and its victims.

Now imagine the story anew. It still begins with a train crash, but you don't know who is injured or killed in the accident. All you know is the *what*: there's a train crash. You must read the story to find out the rest.

And now, dear writer, imagine the story yet again. The train crash still happens, but not until the very end. The reader has spent the story building allegiances to characters and living alongside them in the world the writer has created. The focus of the story has shifted away from the crash, yet it still happens, as a surprise, claiming and sparing the same victims as the previous versions of this story but with a wholly different effect on the reader.

Take a moment to consider the appeal and emotional impact of each story structure. Which version would you most like to read and why? What makes that version preferable to the alternatives? What challenges does each version present for the writer? And for the reader? Do any of these approaches seem manipulative or dishonest in their rendering?

What You Know/ When You Know It

In *12 Years a Slave*, the title alone tells the reader that the author, Solomon Northup, was enslaved for twelve years. Presumably, since Northup lived to recount his experiences, we can also gather that he achieved freedom after those twelve years, at which time he wrote about his experiences of slavery. The dramatic mystery within the book doesn't hinge upon *whether* he achieves freedom, or even when, but how.

Conversely, I provided a structural rewrite for a memoir that was published posthumously. The author was murdered; the notes that comprised her memoir were found after her death. The reader doesn't learn of the author's death until the end of her story, in a postscript provided by the author's mother. I often reflect upon how differently that book would read if the fact of her murder had been disclosed sooner. Ultimately, the book was about her emotional journey from resentment of her mother to peaceful acceptance of their relationship. To preface the narrative with the author's unexpected and tragic fate would fundamentally shift the intention of the author's memoir and distract from that journey toward understanding what she was writing about.

Think about the memoirs in your toolbox and how those writers structured their narratives. Pick one, or a couple, and consider (a) how the writer ordered the events, and (b) how the story would be different had they chosen a different structure.

The "What If" Game

In the previous exercise, you looked at some well-known memoirs, how they're structured, and how they would read if the author had made different narrative choices. Now, let's turn that "what if" wondering to your own memoir. Think over some key points in the story, or maybe even *the* key point—the great dramatic reveal when we learn that you were a spy/a famous artist's muse/the head writer for *Alf*. How would your story change depending on how and when you reveal this information? Would it make your memoir more or less interesting, relatable, moving, or mysterious?

The Big Question(s)

Here's another paradox for you, writer: questions are both essential and disastrous to your story. It all comes down to which questions we're talking about.

Questions can keep a reader engaged and wondering, "what will happen next?" Maybe the narrator's inexplicable motivation is the great mystery of the memoir: why did they abandon the love of their life? On the other hand, the answer to that question could be important to understanding the rest of the memoir and shouldn't be so opaque as to disrupt the narrator's credibility or relatability. As the writer, you walk a fine line between providing enough information for the reader to feel like they have their bearings and understand the story, yet leaving enough work for the reader to keep them engaged and interested.

In this exercise, let's identify those questions you want your reader to have, and those that can be more problematic. Then you can figure out ways to ensure readers have the answers they need and are only asking the awesome, page-turning kind of questions.

In the "Awesome!" column, list those things you *want* your reader to find out throughout the course of the story (think, "Whodunnit?" or "How did you, the best and most-decorated conductor out there, come to crash your train into a herd of cows?" or "When is the narrator going to realize she has toilet paper stuck to her shoe?"). These are the great, necessary questions that keep your reader engaged.

In the "Uncool" column, list those things you don't want your reader puzzling over. (Think, "Does the reader understand why I wanted to become a successful dog walker?" or "Did they get my explanation of how shock collars work?")

Awesome!   **Uncool**

_____   _____
_____   _____
_____   _____
_____   _____
_____   _____
_____   _____
_____   _____

Now that you've listed both the good and gross questions, take some time to consider how you can keep your reader reading to answer the former, but successfully answer the latter so your reader doesn't get confused or frustrated.

_____

_____

_____

_____

_____

_____

_____

_____

_____

_____

_____

_____

_____

_____

_____

_____

_____

_____

_____

_____

_____

_____

_____

_____

Hot tip: Look back at your story scoping graph on page 48. Are there topics or details you could add there from this list of questions? The graph will be helpful in the next chapter, so it would be practical to ensure you've included everything you can think of in your story's scope.

Legendary Moments, Revisited

Back in Chapter 2, you wrote a potential first scene establishing yourself, the author, as both the narrator and main character of this real-life saga. Look back at the scene you chose. Is there anything about the scene you'd change? Or would you pick an entirely different moment to kick off your memoir? Considering what you've been working on over the last chapter, rework this first scene accordingly or pick a different scene altogether and write that instead. Or, if you nailed it on the first try and wouldn't change a thing, turn the music up loud and do a little (or extra-long) victory dance.

Listen up, writer. That chapter was filled with mental gymnastics, and you performed admirably. Even if you're a little sore from it all, you've now considered how to write your memoir for maximum effectiveness and impact. I have one final, and only minimally physical, task for you: choose a hand, any hand; make a fist; look down at your fist such that you can see the side profile of your clenched hand; now punch the sky as hard as you can. You've got it! Let's fist pump our way into Chapter 5.

CHAPTER 5

ORDERING THE EVENTS

CHECKLIST

- [ ] Toolbox
- [ ] Food for Thought with Abigail Thomas
- [ ] Moving Through Space and Time
- [ ] Revelatory Patterns
- [ ] The Time of Your Life
- [ ] Plotlining
- [ ] Pizza Party

For those of you who love to outline (the plotters among us, in NaNo-speak), this is your chapter. You're welcome. And for those "pantsers" who relish the blank page and never fear the unknown, some of the activities here in Chapter 5 might feel a little tortuous. I apologize.

Allow me to explain.

In this chapter you'll create a real-life timeline of events as they happened to you from birth until the present moment as you sit here, reading these words. Thanks to your story sieve and handy scoping graph, you already have a fair idea which of those myriad moments from your life will feature in your memoir. Having an established and complete real-world chronology will help you immensely in planning the order of your story—everything from the distant to more recent past that you're including in your memoir.

As you, the captain of this ship, navigate your story through the waters of your past, your "in real life" timeline will be like your map—a reference to where everything exists in your past. Using that, you can choose the route for your memoir from beginning to middle to The End, resulting in something of an outline for your memoir.

In *Ready, Set, Novel!*, these two timelines were called the Time Machine, populated with the events of your memoir as they fall upon the timeline of your life; and the Plot Machine, representing where the events of your life and the details of your story fall upon a narrative arc that begins with your "Once upon a time"—the first scene in your book—and ends with, you guessed it, living happily ever after. Or unhappily, as the case may be.

I relied heavily on these timelines from *Ready, Set, Novel!* as I wrote my memoir, using tiny Post-it Notes to order and reorder the events on each until I had it just so, and then referencing each as I wrote. I hope these are as useful to you in your plotting, writing, and referencing as they were to me.

If you're feeling anxious about grabbing that ship's wheel and setting sail on the waters of your past, take heart, matey. There are warm-up exercises aplenty to help you plot your path forward.

Give me a "yaaaaaar." C'mon. "YAAAAAAAAAAR!"

Superb. Away we go.

Toolbox

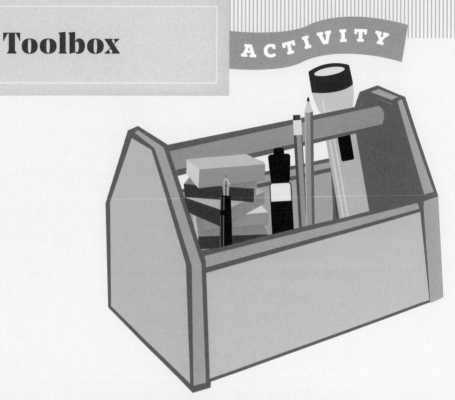

As I mentioned in the intro, Post-its can be massively helpful for this section of memoir plan-ning. You can use the tiny ones, roughly 1.5 × 2 inches (4 × 5 cm), to fill in the timelines in your workbook. Or, once you've done that, and you need more room to write more details and in a larger format, dedicate some blank wall space or a whiteboard and go big! You can put up some butcher paper or put the Post-its directly on the wall or the whiteboard. Or, if you're using a whiteboard and don't have eraser-happy little ones at home, you can just use markers. For this iteration of the timelining, I use the bigger Post-its, ranging from the standard-sized square ones all the way up to the extra-large, 6 × 8 in (roughly 15 × 20 cm) ones. In list form, you might want the following:

- Post-its galore (I bought every size available and used them all.)

- Pencils and/or pens

- Butcher paper and poster-mounting putty or adhesive

- A large whiteboard and whiteboard markers

Food for Thought

"On a dark and stormy night."
"Once upon a time."
"A long time ago and far, far away"

"I am very bored by chronology. I am not interested in every bite of every sandwich chewed and swallowed at lunch. I am just interested in the stuff that has emotional impact for me. There *is* jumping around. I find it so interesting to be somewhere and write that—what's happening now—and then suddenly have a memory of 40 years ago. And that has to fit somewhere, too."

— Abigail Thomas, author of the acclaimed memoirs *A Three Dog Life, Safekeeping: Some True Stories from a Life,* and *What Comes Next and How to Like It*

In the previous chapter you figured out the moments of your life that make for dramatic storytelling—the impactful event that kicks off your story, along with other significant reveals and turning points. Thomas's quote reminds us that there are essentially two timelines at work in a story: the recent past and then the distant past, represented through flashbacks. These two timelines must coexist and support each other in your story, whether you adhere to a chronological retelling of events or, as Thomas suggests, your logic for ordering events is more associative. Together, we'll figure out how to keep your narrative balanced and propulsive at the same time.

Moving Through Space and Time

You might be reading that activity title and thinking, "Like Scott Bakula in *Quantum Leap*?" Or maybe you're more of a *Doctor Who* fan, and you're envisioning a magnificent TARDIS. We're looking at non–sci-fi means of whisking your readers through the many and various events of your life, be they memories from the distant realm of childhood, or the more recent history of yesteryear.

Backgrounding: By using historical events, either in your life or in the wider world, or a combination of both, you set the scene for the personal recollections you'll be writing about at the time. This helps ground the reader in a specific place and time, attaching your narrative to recognizable places and occurrences from a larger and possibly shared cultural tapestry. Think about the opening lines of *Dirty Dancing* (which is neither book nor memoir, nor even nonfiction, but provides a terrific example of the storytelling technique). In voiceover, the main character tells us the year (1963), providing cultural touchstones (pre-Beatles, and Kennedy was still president) while keeping the exposition personal by mentioning her nickname (Baby) and alluding to her hero-worship of her father. That's a lot for one sentence, and it works to ground us immediately in the timeline of the story and give us a sense of who's driving the narrative.

Flashback: If your memoir largely takes places in the more recent past, you may be including select moments from childhood or youth to illustrate certain points about yourself or your family, or to share an impactful or formative experience from that distant time. No need to preface these flashbacks with "I remember"—in fact, it's advisable to avoid that phrase and variations therein unless you're highlighting that your memory of a thing is unreliable. The reader naturally assumes you remember everything in the pages of your memoir.

When integrating flashbacks in your narrative, make sure it's clear that you've shifted from a more recent timeline to the more distant past. Ideally, these anecdotes, scenes, and recollections provide greater insight into you as the narrator and the story you're telling. As Abigail Thomas reminds us, the point is not recalling "every bite of every sandwich chewed and swallowed," but including those illustrative moments that give the story greater meaning and give the reader further relevant information.

Foreshadowing: Hinting at events to come later in the story, foreshadowing can have a mixed effect. It gives a glimpse into the future and also gives certain outcomes away. Strangely, foreshadowing can both undermine a story's suspense factor or increase it—or do both at once—because it will often allude to something that is going to happen but leaves the reader wondering how that event comes to pass. Per the exercise in Chapter 4 about questions that arise in readers' minds, foreshadowing can prompt as many questions as it answers.

Solomon Northup utilizes foreshadowing frequently in *12 Years a Slave*. Of his acquaintance Eliza's fate, he writes in the same chapter in which we first meet her that "Eliza is now dead [. . .] How all her fears were realized—how she mourned day and night, and never would be comforted—how, as she predicted, her heart did indeed break, with the burden of maternal sorrow, will be seen as the narrative proceeds."

From this passage, the reader relinquishes hope that Eliza and her children will remain together; instead, we learn that she dies after protracted misery, though we don't know how or when exactly.

There are many other examples that function similarly, as in Chapter 4, when the slave trader Burch's fate is intimated in the passage reading, "For the present [Burch] disappears from the scenes recorded in this narrative, but he will appear again before its close, not in the character of a man-whipping tyrant, but as an arrested cringing criminal in a court of law, that failed to do him justice." Again, these words are hints and gestures of what is to come, and their narrative function is debatable. It reminds the reader that the writer is all-knowing, doling out parcels of information as he sees fit. To that end, it reinforces the authority of the narrator, even as it breaks the fourth wall and reminds us that we are an audience member in thrall to the memoirist.

How much present-day reflection a writer ought to include, knowing what they know now as they write the events of the past, is debatable and entirely up to your discretion. If you're looking for a way to highlight or emphasize your present knowledge and call attention to your role as author, narrator, *and* character, then adding foreshadowing is a good option.

Flashforward: Like foreshadowing, a flashforward will take the story from its current place in time to a future date, revealing something—perhaps an outcome or opinion from the writer's current viewpoint. As compared to the vague nature and brevity of foreshadowing, flashforwards are more sustained and less ambiguous, providing information that will presumably cast a different light on the events leading up to it. Flashforwards inserted into a narrative taking place primarily in the distant past are a means for the writer to share the wisdom of their experience, overlaying their current perspective on their younger selves and the long-since-passed events they're relating in their memoir.

Revelatory Patterns

Every memoirist's method of incorporating various narrative timelines is so unique as to be like a fingerprint. No two books will move through space and time in quite the same way. In *12 Years a Slave*, almost all references to the distance past are relegated to the first chapter. The rest of the narrative proceeds chronologically except for the occasional and obvious use of foreshadowing. In my memoir, I followed more of a thematically inspired structure, such that each chapter switched back and forth between the distant and recent past, the flashbacks selected based on the theme of the chapter. Other examples might alternate timelines from chapter to chapter, spending one in the distant past before returning in the next section to the more recent narrative timeline. Yet other memoirists may revisit the same point in time over and over, its significance and meaning ever changing as the narrative progresses and more information passes from writer to reader.

I can't tell you what will work best for you—this is one aspect of craft that is strongly tied to instinct and is eminently debatable. What I can suggest is that you take your short stack of well-known memoirs from your Chapter 1 Toolbox and see what patterns you can discern from their pages. Take note of what you observe, and also what you feel works and doesn't work, or what approaches might be appealing for you to try in your own writing.

The Time of Your Life

The time has come to return to that great, detailed graph you completed back in Chapter 3, when you were scoping your story. In this exercise you'll take that wide range of anecdotes, memories, and moments and plot them on the provided timeline according to when they happened in your life and in relation to one another. If you're a visual learner like I am, this will satisfy an itch to "see" your life story in linear fashion.

Unless you are a mental magician, I imagine this timeline will go through many iterations until you get the order of events complete and in correct order. Remember, this isn't your whole life written out on a timeline—only those key moments that feature in your memoir.

TIMELINE

TIMELINE

Plotlining

However much your "IRL" timeline changes throughout the course of its utility, it's nothing compared to how often you're likely to draft, rearrange, change your mind, and redraft this narrative timeline. That's a good thing! I hope you stocked up on Post-its and/or pencils with great erasers so that you can make as many additions and adjustments as you need, as often as you need, until everything falls where it should. Go wild with where you place your flashbacks and any foreshadowing or flashforwards you might choose to incorporate. Play around with which recent events correlate to which portions of your backstory. This is where the theory of the previous chapter gets put into practice; you may be surprised what surprising revelations and dramatic arcs arise out of the combinations you conjure.

Hot tip: If you like a version of plot points you've laid out here, but want to keep playing around with the order, take a photo and save it to your computer with a descriptive title or even some accompanying notes about why this narrative timeline works. Then you can rearrange it without having lost any intel.

YOUR "ONCE UPON A TIME"

YOUR TURNING POINT OR MOMENT OF CHANGE

HOW YOUR STORY ENDS

Another hot tip: If you've plotlined exhaustively and there are still holes, questions, or unresolved story-ordering issues, don't panic! The next chapter is called "Filling in the Blanks," and you'll be doing just that. You can always revisit this—or any—exercise, any time.

Pizza Party

You have reached a major milestone, memoirist. You're more than halfway through this workbook *and* you now have all the information you need to start drafting your memoir. The following chapters will help you fill in some blanks, if there are any; you'll spend some time thinking about revision, once that draft is ready for rewrites; and you'll also come up with some foolproof plans for combatting obstacles that arise in the writing process. But for now, you've done yeoman's work in assembling all the information you need to draft your singular story.

We have a tradition in my house of pizza Friday nights to celebrate the end of another work week. I invite you to join the party. You've done way more than just get from Monday to Friday, so serve yourself a slice and pat yourself on the back while you're at it. And since you've got your pens, pencils, and markers handy, why not go ahead and color in your pizza and party decorations?

CHAPTER 6

FILLING IN
THE BLANKS

CHECKLIST

- [ ] Food for Thought with Brooke Warner
- [ ] Researching Your Life
- [ ] In a World . . .
- [ ] An Emotional Investigation
- [ ] Creating Composites
- [ ] Embracing the Uncertainty

In recent chapters, we have spent quite a bit of time curating the contents of your memoir and carefully excluding those things that neither fit nor belong in your narrative. But what of the things you want to include—things that would move your story forward or provide important backstory—but you don't have a good handle on?

Here in Chapter 6 you'll identify those moments, memories, and details you aren't sure about or can't quite re-create. Nobody expects that you have encyclopedic recall of everything that has ever happened to you, how it happened, what you or someone else might have said, and all the other exact details of your life that fade with time. Readers will expect you to be truthful in your recounting of events from your life, though, so what gives? How can we be authentic about things we can't perfectly replicate?

Intention, motivation, impressions, and honesty are all critical in your efforts to write the events and interactions included in your memoir. There are also a number of tips and tricks you can employ to help you locate details and context you may have forgotten about or didn't even know you had access to. In the activities that follow, you'll do some deep dives in the past for the treasures you might've thought were lost forever but may have been hiding just out of sight. You will also explore the mysteries of composite characters and scenes and try your hand at creating some of your own. These composites may help your story, or you may find you're better off without them.

There will still be undiscoverable gems from years gone by that you can't in good conscience include, and that's okay, too. The biggest takeaway should be how you bring the past to life with integrity, accuracy, and a fullness that benefits your story. I'd wager you will be well pleased with everything you're able to retrieve from the vaults of time.

Food for Thought

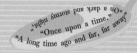

"On a dark and stormy night."
"Once upon a time,"
"A long time ago and far, far away"

"In memoir, as in any genre, it's allowed—
encouraged, even—to create composites of
people, of scenes. No memoir, in my opinion,
is pure truth since you don't live your life
with a tape recorder strapped to your belt.
Your truth lies in the interpretation of your
experiences and so to me, truth is authenticity,
but truth is also integrity. It's telling things like
they actually would have gone, even if you have
to piece together some of the memories without
manipulation and without trying to look better
than you are, without grandstanding."

— Brooke Warner, publisher of She Writes Press and author of *Write On, Sisters!*

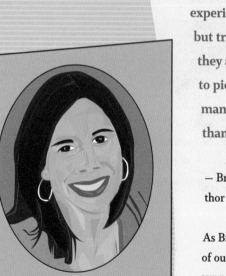

As Brooke says, we can't possibly remember every aspect
of our lives exactly as it happened. However, evidence of
our past is plentiful if we get creative and know where to
look. Investigating your life can help you remember things
you might have forgotten and help you fill in scenes, conversations, and descriptions with precision.

Researching Your Life

It's possible that your memoir predates much of the technology we now rely upon. I was still using a flip phone and posting to Friendster and Myspace in the recent-past timeframe I wrote about in my memoir. My childhood was in the early-'80s era of dot matrix printers and Oregon Trail, but I was still able to excavate some real gems from those distant days. No matter what years your memoir spans, some of these resources would surely help you retrieve valuable information you might've thought was lost forever.

- Email

- Letters

- Text messages/chat apps

- Social media accounts

- Journals

- Photographs (digital or analog—I was able to look at old family slides, but maybe you have some old film negatives saved somewhere!)

- Home videos or digital recordings

- Audio recordings

- Friends' and family's memories or written accounts

- Memory boxes or scrap books

- Heirlooms and keepsakes

- Medical records

- Genealogy websites

- Public records

- Birth/death/wedding announcements

What other resources could you draw upon to fill in the blanks of your story and provide details that might otherwise be a little fuzzy? Use the space here to make your own list of leads you might pursue and the evidence you uncover. Perhaps you're able to recall a favorite article of clothing, rediscover a turn of phrase you or someone else used a lot, or stumble across an important written exchange. You never know where a crucial detail might be lurking!

If you still need more emotional and experiential evidence, try some of these activities.

Reflect on the things you'd do for fun during the times you write about. Watch a movie—or several—that you loved. Read your favorite book. Play your favorite board game. Long-buried associations may surface, releasing memories and emotions you'd forgotten about.

Make a playlist. Think about the music from the time or times you're writing about to make a soundtrack populated with significant songs.

Remember your hobbies. If you had one or more hobbies at that time, try your hand at whatever you were into—or even those things you weren't into but were compelled to practice. Whether it was horseback riding, working on cars, making friendship bracelets, skipping stones, stamp collecting, playing the piano or other instrument or sport, or speaking a foreign language, accessing that latent muscle memory could be very revealing.

Make a meal. Or make many meals of your favorite foods from that time or, if not your favorites, the things you ate a lot. For example, many of my meals in the time of my memoir consisted of free samples from the grocery store. Try to recall what you were snacking on, cooking, or being forced to eat at the family dining table.

Naturally, if any of your favorite pastimes were dangerous to yourself or others, please don't revisit them. There are plenty of alternative memory experiences (listen to that music! Watch that movie!) that are healthy and safe and will have a terrific memory-generating effect.

Note any other activities you might try.

_____

_____

_____

_____

_____

_____

_____

83

In a World. . .

In addition to sorting the particulars of your past, it's equally important to ground your story in the place and time—or multiple places and time periods—you're writing about. Just as it can be difficult to remember exactly what was happening in your life at various moments, it can be challenging to recall what was happening in the world. There are several resources you can access to paint a complete picture of your setting and the current events in the time span you're recalling. For example, I used the following to fill in missing or scant detail in my memoir:

- *Farmers' Almanac*
- Google Maps (especially street view!)
- Google searching dates and places
- Newspaper articles
- Library archives
- Visiting actual locations, when possible

It's amazing what feelings of recognition or nostalgia some armchair travel can inspire. If this list of suggestions still leaves you without a rich sense of place and time, try some of the following memory-triggering exercises:

Note any location-specific details you unearthed in the previous activity's investigations. Look for clues about seasonal climate, landmarks that are since demolished, local traditions, or defining features of the regional landscape.

_____

_____

_____

_____

_____

_____

_____

_____

_____

_____

_____

Research cultural touchstones in the years you're writing about. For instance, pay attention to cultural award winners (Pulitzers, Nobel Peace Prize, Academy Awards, World Series or Super Bowl champs, Olympics highlights) as well as any big criminal trials, political scandals, natural disasters, fads (think bell bottoms, scrunchies, Beanie Babies, trolls, fidget spinners), trends, major technological advancements or achievements, global conflicts or crises, or anything at all that influenced the collective consciousness.

_____

_____

_____

_____

_____

_____

_____

_____

_____

Read up on existing literature about the place, time period, or subject matter you're covering in your memoir. This could include other nonfiction, informational websites or fictional stories set in the same time/place that you're writing about. Having the correct vocabulary for the flora and fauna of a region, weather patterns, cultural movements, or rituals helps tremendously in writing a specific recounting. Spending mental time in those spaces, too, will likely refresh your own memory.

_____

_____

_____

_____

_____

_____

_____

_____

_____

Of course, you're not beholden to include these details in your story. These exercises will likely serve to better inform your descriptions and recollections, while helping you to write from a memory-rich perspective that will doubtless infuse your memoir with confidence and atmospheric accuracy.

An Emotional Investigation

What about those things in your memoir that can't be visited or researched—like feelings or impressions? I'd argue those can be accessed, too, but you won't need to pull down any boxes or even open a browser window. You may already have triggered some of those old, intangible emotions in the previous activities. Here a few more investigative maneuvers you might want to try that require nothing more than closing your eyes and concentrating.

Think about a character you write about in your memoir. How might the other person have felt at the time of life that they appear in your story? What was their motivation to do the things they did? What were their needs, wants, fears, weaknesses, and strengths at that time?

_____

_____

_____

_____

_____

_____

What were your own needs, wants, fears, weaknesses, and strengths? Did you have a recurring nightmare? Any persistent phobias? Did you win any awards or receive any accolades you can recall? Was there a particular disagreement you had with a friend, partner, or family member (or even a stranger!) that was fraught with greater meaning about who you were at that time?

_____

_____

_____

_____

_____

_____

_____

_____

_____

_____

Think about how you will portray various scenes. What will be portrayed through dialogue? Exposition? Allusion? Conjecture?

_____

_____

_____

_____

_____

_____

_____

_____

_____

_____

_____

_____

_____

_____

_____

_____

_____

For those passages that re-create written communications you no longer have access to, try to re-create the specificity of their word choices, verbosity, or any quirks in their writing style. Ideally, you have other samples of their writing that will help you hone in on their unique tones and rhythms of written expression.

_____

_____

_____

_____

_____

_____

Make notes as you go to preserve the nuances and minutiae of the evidence you uncover. Nailing dialogue and written exchanges can be tricky, but a little empathy, observation, and practice can go a long way toward rendering an emotionally authentic portrayal of the people in your memoir and the communication you had with them.

Creating Composites

As we learned in this chapter's Food for Thought, memoirists can create composites for scenes and characters. What is a composite, you may be wondering? Whether we are talking scene or character composites, you are taking multiples of something— supporting characters or different moments, for example—and collapsing them into one. Why do that? In the space of a book-length work, you likely won't have time to explain all the frogs you've kissed, all the friends you've had, and all the relevant communication you've had with each of them.

Trying to give each person in your life who contributed to your story their own space on the page, with enough description and significance to warrant their presence as a character, could make for a very long and unwieldy list of cameos that cause continuity-editing nightmares for you and confuse your reader. Instead you can simplify both your writerly responsibilities and your readers' understanding of the story by imbuing one character with the contributions of many.

When it comes to scene composites, think of a series of conversations you may have had with your mom, or a boss, or a neighbor, or anyone over a span of time—it could be all the questions you've ever asked your magic mirror on the wall. Instead of establishing the timeframe and setting for each exchange—maybe one was a text, one was over lunch, and one was over the course of several phone calls—you as the writer and master editor can extract the most important things that were written or said and sum them up in a single, streamlined exchange. If the gist of the conversation remains the same, and the emotional truth of it is unchanged, there is no harm in condensing a series of exchanges, occurring in various locations over a span of time, into one continuous scene.

I don't pretend to have all the answers for how this is done in every scenario, but here are some helpful guidelines to abide by when consolidating characters or scenes in your story:

- Is the essential information imparted to the reader the same before and after you created the composite?
- Are you still sharing the emotional truth of the communication with honesty and integrity to yourself and the other people involved?
- Will having fewer scenes and characters in your memoir make it easier to read and understand?
- Did everything occurring in a composite scene actually happen at some point in time? And are all the actions and communications of characters represented in a composite attributable to actions and communications of people in your life?

If the answer to these questions is yes, you're in great shape. If, however, fundamental truths about yourself or your life are getting skewed in the process, or your internal BS-o-meter is shrieking, stop what you're doing and reassess. You may find that upon further examination, places where you thought you needed to use composites don't call for it after all.

One way to consider the composites you create involves a simple but handy graph like the one below, where the axes are accuracy and readability. Ideally, your composite scenes should remain true *and* enhance the readability or ease of understanding, such that—when plotted—your composites fall on or dang close to the line. This chart helps outside of the composite-scene conversation as well; you can do a spot check throughout your memoir to ensure that what you're writing isn't 100% accurate but impenetrably complicated or confusing to anyone that isn't you, or that you've written a humdinger—a real tear-jerking page-turner—but it's based loosely on real-life events.

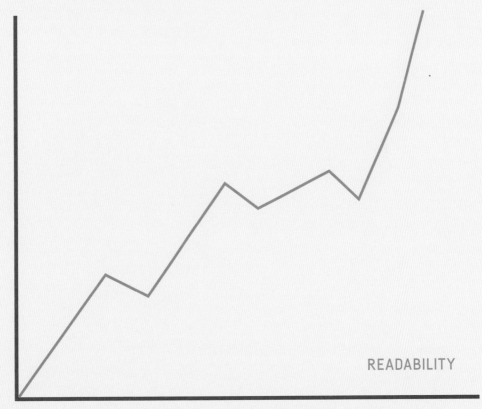

ACCURACY

READABILITY

If, after prolonged agonizing, you're still uncertain about the endlessly debatable vagaries of truth in representation, the next chapter has even more exercises to help you toe the line of authenticity.

Embracing the Uncertainty

As much as you research and reflect on the past and produce realistic answers to bridge the gaps in your memory, you won't have a solution to or reason for everything. Neither will your reader expect you to. In fact, proclaiming too much certainty can backfire and come off as inauthentic. Some ambiguity and lingering questions are important to memoir, for they also represent the truth of memory, which is, in its essence, episodic, incomplete, and impression-istic. With that in mind, what unanswered questions or vague recollections can you leave well enough alone?

You dug deep and did some great investigative work over the course of this chapter. I hope you feel rewarded by your efforts and are at peace with those things that remain out of reach. Take comfort in the words of Holmes himself, who said, "What one man can invent, another can discover." Here's to you, gumshoe, and your readiness to eschew invention in favor of that which is discoverable. It will serve your story well.

CHAPTER 7
REST, RESET, REVISE!

CHECKLIST

- ☐ Time Out
- ☐ A Food for Thought Feast
- ☐ Your (Pay)checklist
- ☐ Quality Control
- ☐ Cut/Keep
- ☐ Reader Readiness

Revision takes energy, concentration, discipline, and time. It is important to celebrate your first draft *and* rest your brain before embarking on this next leg of the memoir-writing journey. Before you set off into the realm of revision, you'll feast on an extra-large helping of Food for Thought, featuring a smorgasbord of wisdom, tips, and tricks you might try when cleaning up your own memoir. I hope they give you a shot of the creative carbs you'll need to complete the exercises in this chapter.

The most important thing you can possibly keep in mind throughout this process is that you've got to tackle any changes from big to small. Make sure the emotional integrity of your memoir is intact before fussing about chapter titles (or your memoir's title!). Don't get hung up on word choice or typos before addressing any structural issues. You'll likely have some boulder-moving to do before you fill in the gaps and cracks, right? I know how fun it is to disappear in a thesaurus for a day—it's my happy place, too—but save your style guide bubble-bathing until after you've done the dirty work.

When you've done the necessary work of polishing your memoir to a high shine, we'll address next big steps, like sharing your work with readers.

Time Out

Writer, you completed the first draft of your memoir! Have you celebrated this truly laudable accomplishment? And have you celebrated it sufficiently? Have you baked (or simply bought) and eaten an entire cake? Slept for an age? Binge-watched all the shows? Showered and changed your clothes? Checked in with friends and family to let them know you're slaying it in the memoir-writing sector?

I ask not just because these are all great and fun things to do, and you definitely deserve to do some prolonged self-congratulating, but also because you need a break from your memoir before you start revising—long enough to gain some new perspective, but not so long that you forget about this worthy project and move on to something else. Long enough, say, to eat a cake, do a month's worth of laundry, and make your streaming subscription pull its weight. For some, this equals a week—maybe more, maybe less. You be the judge. If you love making (and crossing out) to-do lists as much as I do, make one here for your celebratory goings-on.

_____

_____

_____

_____

_____

_____

_____

_____

_____

_____

_____

_____

_____

_____

_____

_____

_____

_____

When you're refreshed and can look at your project with a clear head and some newly established distance, begin this chapter and the revision phase of writing your memoir.

Ready? Set! Revise away, memoirist. You've got this.

A Food for Thought Feast

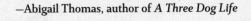

"A long time ago and far, far away"
"Once upon a time."
"On a dark and stormy night."

"Allow yourself to write badly and not throw it away—just keep going—because the way we learn is to do it wrong, and then do it a little less wrong. Never throw out your first draft because that's where the fire is. Even if the words are gonna change, that's where the fire is. And you have to go back to that and catch on again. You have to allow yourself to write badly before you can write well."

—Abigail Thomas, author of *A Three Dog Life*

"My first attempts were more therapy than writing a book for other people. [. . .] I was way too close to my own hurt, and too in love with my own victimhood, and my book didn't have a higher purpose or meaning or reason. There was no paycheck for the reader."

—Meredith May, author of *The Honey Bus: A Memoir of Loss, Courage and a Girl Saved by Bees*

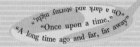

"Using my mom as the recipient of [*Heavy*] helped me decide what I was going to cut because she always has to be there in some form or fashion. I used my mom to guide the revision process in terms of what I was going to cut and what I was going to keep."

—Kiese Laymon, author of *Heavy: An American Memoir*

"In the middle of writing my memoir, *Good Talk*, I realized that
I didn't have the perspective of remove, nor was I going to be
suddenly objective before I needed to turn the book in. No, I was
in the middle of this thing and it was going to be really painful to
try to write the truth of it, not to mention tricky. How do you not
just constantly defend yourself? How do you not just come down
on your own side? How do you intellectually, rigorously question
where you're coming from in the same moment when you feel
like all you want to do is have your own back? That's when line
between clarity and vindication became really, really important
to me. With every finished chapter, I would ask myself, *Are you
writing the hard truth of this moment? And if you are, are you
writing it for clarity or vindication?* And then I would sit with
that, sometimes for days. My basic rule was, if you're writing it
for vindication, you have to cut it; if you're writing it for clarity,
you get to keep it."

—Mira Jacob, author of *Good Talk:
A Memoir in Conversations*

Your (Pay)checklist

In her Food for Thought, Meredith May calls the larger purpose of her memoir—outside of its personal utility—the "paycheck." This is the reason a reader should pick up your book. Think about your memoir's "higher purpose, meaning, or reason," as Meredith says. Does it have any (or all) of these? Note your thoughts here, along with those places you think your book nails it, and those places where you're still writing for more therapeutic reasons.

_____

_____

_____

_____

_____

_____

_____

_____

_____

_____

_____

_____

_____

_____

_____

_____

_____

_____

_____

_____

_____

_____

_____

_____

_____

_____

_____

_____

_____

_____

_____

Writing itself is therapeutic, so the more you write and rewrite and revise, the more your story scale will tip away from the "seeking catharsis" end of the spectrum and toward that larger reason for sharing your story.

Quality Control

You may be starting to see that revision isn't a single pass through your memoir to make sure everything makes sense and you haven't committed a there/their/they're gaffe. Instead, it's a multifaceted assessment of your story's composition. Here are some highlights you'll want to hit as you refine your first draft (and your fifth, six, seventh, and beyond).

Accuracy: Have you faithfully represented the truth as you lived it? You'll know deep in your gut if the answer is no. And your reader probably will, too. If you're still exaggerating portions of the story for effect, casting events that happened to others as your own experience, or fabricating those things you can't remember, you can either rework those sections to cleave more faithfully to reality, or you may decide you're more comfortable writing this as fiction instead.

Emotional Truth: Motivation check! If there are places where your objective is defending yourself, vilifying another, making anyone seem like something they're not, or anything that reads remotely like score-settling, do as Mira Jacob did and draw a line between that which moves the story forward and that which serves an ulterior motive.

Focus: Look at your original Venn diagram, showing what your memoir is fundamentally about. Have you hewn to that subject matter, or did you stray off course at some point? It may be that as another aspect of your memoir's focus slipped—whether it was emotional, factual, or otherwise—so did the thematic continuity. Fear not: This is what revision is for!

Structural Viability: Does your memoir read like a story? Is there a clear beginning, middle, and end? A reason for the reader to care what happens? Do you, the main character and narrator, change over the course of the narrative? Do you lose or gain anything? Again, if your story is a little flat and boring, don't freak out. Drafts are drafts for a reason! Return to Chapter 4 and see if perhaps reordering your narrative might raise the intrigue. Or pull a memoir off the shelf to see how that writer kept you turning the pages.

Correctness: Only at the very end of the revision process, when you've kept what belongs and cut the dreck, when everything is in the right place and you're ready to think about sharing your story with readers, should you do your close line edits for typos and grammatical correctness. *Now* you may worry over word choice. Enjoy—you've earned it.

Cut/Keep

Mira Jacob's rule was, "If you're writing it for vindication, you have to cut it; if you're writing it for clarity, you get to keep it." Kiese Laymon's cut/keep guideline was his mother and her presence in his narrative. Now you will determine what your rule or guideline will be. This will help you tremendously in ensuring quality control of the story metrics listed in the previous exercise. Maybe you'll end up with a few guidelines by which you edit. Grab a pencil, erasable pen, or tiny Post-its and see what works for you. When you've figured it out, write it in ink and recite it like a mantra.

If it's _____, cut it; if it's _____, keep it.

As you come across places in your memoir that run afoul of your guideline, don't just select and delete them. Instead, make a list here with a brief summary of each scene and its location in your memoir (page number will suffice). Then, consider for each:

What do you lose by cutting this sentence/paragraph/scene entirely? For example, is there important information imparted, even though its done in a way that doesn't quite jibe with your theme or the strictures of truth-telling?

Is there meaning to be salvaged from the scene? If so, how could you recast it to be more accurate, honest, or in line with your cut/keep guideline?

In short, if there's value in the passages you've listed here, don't just cut them straightaway, but instead try to rework them so the essential information is preserved in a way that strengthens your story.

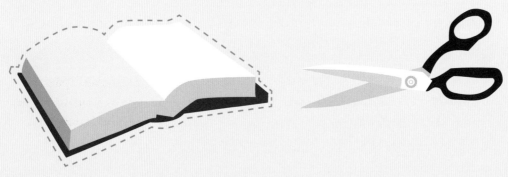

Location	Description	Notes

Reader Readiness

Have you done all the things? Did you do the thing you should never do and name your draft "final"? Well, get ready to start numbering your final drafts, because it's about time to share your "final" draft with readers.

Before you do that, though, read your book aloud to yourself. You'll be astonished how much this last act will catch, including but not limited to:

- Overlong or confusing sentences

- Repetition of words or phrases

- Overuse of adverbs or unnecessary adjectives

- Stilted dialogue

- Sneaky lurking typos

Once you've remedied those last lingering stylistic and formatting issues, then—and only then—should you start looking for volunteers to read your book. Seek these individuals out with the following in mind:

Who: Don't just ask people who will love everything about the book because they love *you*. You're welcome to include them in the reader pool, but don't expect revelatory critiques from them. Neither should you seek someone who would expect to be paid for their time—you may seek a professional's opinion in time, but not yet. Instead, find a few middle-ground types: book-loving souls you think would be happy to provide honest feedback and be able to do so in a timely manner. This could be a friend or a colleague, a writing group acquaintance, or someone you know from an online forum.

What: Be clear about what you need from them. If you don't ask for specific feedback, they probably won't give you specific feedback. Make a list of questions, for example, that you have about their experience of your work, seeking information that would help you further refine your memoir. For example, "What were you curious to learn more about? Was that curiosity ultimately satisfied? What confused you? Was there an outcome you hoped for? Were your expectations confounded? Did you feel like anything was misleading or missing?" Customize this list to be specific to your story and characters and to suit your needs.

When: Set a realistic deadline for feedback. Give your readers long enough to read with care, but not so long that they'll completely forget to do it. I have found that, depending on the circumstance, anywhere from one to three months is fair. Ideally, they will tell you how long they need and then stick to it.

How: Whether you're asking in person or in writing, make sure you're clear in your requests and expectation, and don't forget to express gratitude for their time and opinions. Clarify with each writer how they should share their suggestions: in writing on a hard copy; digitally, by tracking changes and inserted comments; in a shared Google document; or otherwise. It may be that they have software constraints and you'll need to find a compromise. Be flexible but clear so neither of you has any lingering questions. Confusion in service to politeness only serves to slow everyone down.

Why: This test run will help you immeasurably in determining what, if anything, turns a reader off, leads them astray, rings false, or triggers any number of other red flags that need addressing. Getting a handful of readers to help you out in this way will also provide you with sample size large enough to show whether a reader's reaction is a one-off or a more widely held opinion.

Think of a small but heartfelt way to thank your readers. Of course, mentioning them in your acknowledgments is a lovely gesture, should you go on to publish. Before that, though, and soon after they provide you with input, give them a token of your appreciation.

What next?
What does one do with a fully revised, reader-vetted manuscript? Turn to The Resource Room (Chapter 9) for more information on writer platform and marketing, as well as recommended books on seeking representation and publication. Experts abound on these "what next" subjects, some of whom have shared their advice within these pages. Seek their wisdom!

CHAPTER 8

OVERCOMING THE INEVITABLE

CHECKLIST

- ☐ (Another) Food for Thought Feast
- ☐ Identifying Your Obstacle
- ☐ Facing Your Fears (Again)
- ☐ Time Generator
- ☐ Busting Writer's Block
- ☐ Creating a Community
- ☐ Lost and Found

Distractions, emergencies, setbacks, surprises, roadblocks, and more will come at you throughout your creative career. Some of them are specific to your writing, and others pertain more to the challenges of "adulting"—unavoidable nuisances that befall us grown-ups and pull us away from our passion projects. It's near impossible to predict the latter category's endless array of unwelcome irritants that will arise while you're trying to complete your memoir. Raccoons in the wall, fires at work (both literal and figurative), kid vomit, cat vomit . . . stuff happens, and we are obligated to deal with it. The former variety of obstacles, though—the ones that pertain to your writing—are well-documented and, I'm happy to report, slightly easier to predict. The fewer problems you're wrestling with, the more time you'll have to make a memoir, so this is where we'll focus our obstacle-busting efforts.

Just because we can get proactive with your memoir maladies doesn't mean these roadblocks don't feel painful and scary. To begin this process, I recruited a bevy of published memoirists to share their struggles and solutions with you in a super-sized Food for Thought. There's comfort in hearing about others' experiences and what has worked for them; many of the activities that follow are modelled on our experts' wisdom. Whether you're grappling with fear of judgment and reprisals (both from within and without); an inability to make time; plain, old-fashioned writer's block; needing but lacking a writing community; or if you're seeking a way out of the woods when you feel utterly lost within your own story, you're in excellent hands.

Before we tackle your memoir-writing issues with expert examples in mind, there is something we can do—two things, really—to ward off disaster. First, keep a fire extinguisher close, because you never know. If you don't have one, buy one. I'll wait. And second, save your manuscript early and often. Whether you email it to yourself or anyone else at the end of the day, put it on a USB stick, or send it up to a cloud, make sure you're keeping an updated copy somewhere in case of a computer-related catastrophe.

Now, let's play some writer's block–inspired Whack-A-Mole!

(Another) Food for Thought Feast

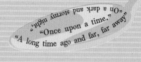

"On a dark and stormy night."
"Once upon a time."
"A long time ago and far, far away"

"What made it worthwhile for me to tell a difficult, embarrassing, in some cases shameful story about my own life was the belief that that vulnerability might create a connection [and] a greater recognition of our common humanity."

—Piper Kerman, on writing
Orange Is the New Black

"It is a brave act to write, and I think if you face those fears or scary places and explore them in the writing with some support— whatever that might be that you need (NaNoWriMo is a good one!), but could also be one person in your life that can be supportive (a friend, a therapist, a parent, a partner) if you're able to do that, I think it's worth it, and the work that comes out of it can not only feel cathartic to the writer but also to other people who read the work."

—Francesca Lia Block, author of *The Thorn Necklace: Healing Through Writing and the Creative Process*

"The pen is your pickaxe, chiseling away at whatever lies between yourself and the deeper truth."

—Dani Shapiro, author of *Inheritance: A Memoir of Genealogy, Paternity, and Love*

"If you're gonna lose people around (publishing your memoir), they were probably people you were going to lose otherwise. If you're writing well and you're being generous (as compassionate as possible in your writing, which is something you *must* do as a memoirist) then if a person takes such offense, it was probably a relationship that was either not good already or was going to be lost anyway."

—Kerry Cohen, author of *Lush* and *The Truth of Memoir: How to Write about Yourself and Others with Honesty, Emotion, and Integrity*

 **ACTIVITY**

Identifying Your Obstacle

Dani Shapiro's Food for Thought urges us to wield our pen against that which is keeping us from our deeper truth. This obstacle could be anything, but in order to write honestly, you've got to overcome it. Before we get into this chapter's tips and tricks for combating common creative stumbling blocks, take a moment to identify your biggest challenge. Have you got it? Can you, intrepid miner of memories, pledge to raise your pen against this narrative nemesis? If and when you're ready to commit, use that same mighty pen to make it official and binding. No take backs!

I, _____(name)_____, do hereby swear to use my pen

against the obstacle of _____(obstacle)_____

in the service of accessing my deeper truth and writing a fully realized memoir.

Facing Your Fears (Again)

Way back in Chapter 2, we faced and vanquished those persistent and occasionally paralyzing anxieties that strike when you're getting vulnerable with your writing, and when you're writing about real-life people whose opinions you care about (or whose judgment you live in fear of). The further into drafting your memoir you get, the more specific, the more real and outsized, these anxieties can get. Even wielding your pen against the most nagging worries can feel futile at times, though you bravely press on. If and when you start feeling distressed, harassed, harangued, or downright panicky, whether it's stemming from your inner editor or the perceived external audience that may one day read your book, it's important to stop those doubting voices before they stop you from writing your truth.

Maybe you already have a mantra to interrupt negative thought patterns and give yourself the confidence you need to get back on track with your writing. Mine was, "If it's true, it's not a problem. And if it *is* a problem, it's *their* problem, not my problem." Even if you're borrowing from *The Little Engine That Could,* such a simple phrase as "I think I can, I think I can" can (and *will!*) help you out of the bad place and back into the light.

Here, too, are a few FAQs to help reassure you and keep you firmly in that safe space, full of confidence and self-possession.

What if the people I am writing about get angry at me? Or if readers judge me and my story?
They might! And, to quote my own personal mantra, I can't control every person's reaction to my experiences. Neither can you. The important thing is that your book cleaves to *your* experience and *your* truth—and you're entitled to both, regardless of anyone else's opinion. Ask yourself early if you're being generous and compassionate in your writing, which, as Kerry Cohen reminds us, we must be. Not everyone will agree with your version of past events, and not everyone has to like your representation of them in writing. If you're writing from a place of openness and honesty, chances are good that your readers will respect you and your version of history, even if they don't love or agree with it, and you really can't ask for more than that.

What if no one reads my book?

This, dear writer, is out of your control for many reasons. Even if you write the best memoir on record and launch an ironclad marketing campaign, it's impossible to know how many people will ultimately buy and read your book. The important thing is that, however many people lay eyes on your story, they're reading the best version of your story you could possibly produce. My memoir sales were abysmal, but the emails and testimonials I received from readers that related to or benefited from my experience have been priceless to me. Focus on the integrity of your storytelling. That's where you have power and influence, so wield it!

What if, after all this time and effort, my book is still a stinking garbage heap?

Please turn back to page 97 and reread Abigail Thomas's Food for Thought. Every first draft is flawed—and yes, maybe some first drafts are so flawed as to resemble a garbage heap, but this is what revision, persistence, and belief are for. Never forget that you are here because you have a story to write. It won't be finished and perfected without considerable effort, and you are absolutely up to the task. You can go the distance. You *will* go the distance!

In the meantime, I want you to hug your garbage heap. Yep, you read that right. Hug away! You made it, it's yours, and it's a crucial part of the journey toward your final draft. Embrace the process, stench and all, and never ever ever give up. But maybe take a shower before turning the page.

Time Generator

We all have at least one way of wasting time that we truly excel at. I am not talking about your run-of-the-mill waffling about what to wear in the morning or lingering over the morning paper. I am talking about the thing you could do for hours even though it feels like you've been checked out for only twenty minutes. Is it Instagramming your day in a 500-part story? Or watching funny hamster videos? Or sweet, simple sleeping in? Mine is playing the *New York Times* word game Beehive in the bath. I could spend hours in the tub trying to reach Genius level.

So, come on, out with it. What is your thing? _____

Bingo. That is your incentive for a successful writing session. You set your writing goal, and when you hit it, allow yourself to indulge in your favorite guilty pleasure—perhaps for thirty minutes.

In addition to incentivizing your time suck, there are other methods of reclaiming hours in your day for writing. Try any or all of these and see how wide open your schedule becomes.

Trade chores for a month: See if your kid or your partner will take on the dog walking, laundry folding, dinner prepping, or other duties that usually fall to you. If they'll cover your chores while you're drafting your memoir, promise to take on their loads (plus your original responsibilities) the following month.

Loosen your standards: Can you let the cleanliness of your house (and clothes, car, dog, and maybe even your children) slide even slightly from their usual maintenance? If you worry about these roughly half as much as usual, you'll be banking major minutes over the course of a month. And in the long run, what's a shaggier-than-usual dog or dustier-than-usual bookshelf when you've got a memoir to show for it?

Time is money: If you're in a position to, have your groceries delivered at least some of the time; buy ready-made meals a few times a week; or pay someone else—maybe a local teenager looking for work—to help you mow the lawn, wash the windows, or babysit for a couple of hours. Alternatively, you could pause those more expensive and time-burning indulgences (think salon services, eating out, weekly dry cleaning) so you're saving time *and* money.

Play Tetris with your calendar: If you're anything like me, interruptions are the death of focus. In those weeks when I know I have a lot to get done, I try to cluster my obligations or known distractions. If I can keep all phone calls, deliveries, meal prep, and house maintenance to the morning hours, leaving the afternoon free for writing, I am setting myself up for success. Look at your calendar to see how you can reorder your days to keep multiple, continuous hours protected for your project.

If you have other clever time-saving tactics, jot them here. Happy time-hunting!

Busting Writer's Block

I attended a writers' conference once where the keynote speaker, a well-known novelist, claimed she tied herself to her office chair and wasn't allowed to get up until she'd logged her hours at the computer. I have never tried this myself, but I've always admired this writer's dedication to the craft and resistance to all excuses. If you're looking for some ways to combat lethargy and stimulate your medulla oblongata that don't involve rope, look no further. (Warning: Some of these will take you away from your desk. If you're venturing away from your workspace, be ready to jot down all the great ideas you generate where and when it's possible to do so!)

Listen to inspirational music: I mentioned in Chapter 1 that I can really boost my word count when listening to stirring movie scores. My husband's work music of choice has to be devoid of lyrics, and it sounds a lot like elevator music to me. Whatever works, right? When you find your ideal music for memoir-making, save a writing playlist on Spotify or iTunes so it's ready and waiting when you sit down to write.

Take a shower: I don't know why it works, but it does. You probably already know this. If you don't, try it!

Go for a walk: Like taking a shower, there's something alchemical in getting your blood pumping just the right amount while doing an otherwise mindless activity. If you're able to, record your brainstorms with a voice memo, so you don't have to stop and take notes every time you have a breakthrough.

Do a puzzle: I don't know why this works either, but it is my favorite mindless method for shaking off brain fog. (I should note that this, and any other activity listed here, should be done unaccompanied and free from distractions to reap the maximum creative inspiration.)

Free-write: If, despite your best efforts, nothing is coming, don't just sit there and stare down the blank page in agony. Write about anything at all—what you can hear or see or smell in the moment, something unusual that happened recently, or something based on a writing prompt (just search "writing prompt" for a plethora of free options). Getting your fingers and brain warmed up on something inconsequential will help you ease into the real work that awaits you.

Leave yourself an "in": When you knock off at the end of a writing session, leave yourself instructions on where to begin and any low-hanging fruit—scenes in progress or unexplored ideas ready to be pursued. Some people might feel itchy leaving loose ends for themselves to pick up at a later time, but this can be a great way to get going quickly every time you sit down with your story.

Have a treat: In the Time Generator exercise, you converted a time-suck activity into a treat for writing. Think of some other, admittedly smaller, incentives that you can space throughout your day to enjoy during a mini-break from dutifully pounding the keyboard. Mine include grabbing another cup of coffee, collecting the mail from downstairs, making lunch, checking the vegetables in the porch garden for new sprouts, reading my email, allowing myself five minutes of scrolling through the news, and afternoon snack time. What would your list look like?

Creating a Community

In her Food for Thought, Francesca Lia Block touched on the importance of a support system to writing, especially if you're grappling with the emotional toll of writing a memoir with intense subject matter. By virtue of your job or your particular situation (maybe you're an MFA student, or you work, like I did, at a literary nonprofit that encourages aspiring writers of all ages to draft their manuscript in a month. . .), you may not have to look very hard to find a creative community. Take advantage of those connections!

For those without an obvious place to turn for creative support, here are some suggestions on where to start. It's a worthy search, and I hope you're able to find your people in short order. They'll help you through the hard parts, troubleshoot the sticky bits, celebrate the high points, and write quietly alongside you—virtually or in-person—when all you need is an accountability partner. (This is also an excellent means of sourcing volunteer readers, as covered in Chapter 7!)

NaNoWriMo: I am mentioning this again, not to belabor the point, but because even writers who have participated in NaNoWriMo for years aren't aware that there are robust, year-round conversations taking place in the forums, as well as in-person events occurring in regional chapters organized by local volunteers called Municipal Liaisons (MLs). You can learn more about both virtual and real-life events on the website, www.nanowrimo.org.

Post a flyer: Is there a community board at work or school where you and your cohorts can communicate about extracurriculars? Maybe this is a Slack channel or an actual cork board in the kitchen. Either way, post a note or start a thread to see if there are other writers around who'd like to start a group for swapping work, writing together, or providing some other form of creative support. You might be surprised how many fellow scribes are hiding in plain sight!

Additionally, or alternatively, inquire or advertise your interest at your local library or favorite bookstore. You may even have luck at your nearby independent coffeehouse, a popular location for such meetups.

Online writing groups: There are so many online resources, it'll make your head spin. (It makes my head spin.) I am limiting my suggestions to those resources I have personally vetted and benefited from.

● Check out local writer groups on www.meetup.com. They're not paying me to say so—I had good success meeting like-minded people this way when I moved many years ago and needed to find a new literary network in my new home.

● If you have a Facebook account, search for active and appealing online communities you'd like to join. NaNoWriMo has one! I am also a member of a local one for readers and writers— the local nature of this group is great because I have access to both the online and in-person offerings. Ideally, you'll find a well-moderated group that monitors membership to verifiable humans and encourages inclusive and supportive discourse on writing. Don't hesitate to leave any groups that are troll-ridden or that don't suit your specific needs.

If you're anything like me (and many other writers out there), you probably wouldn't characterize yourself as "extroverted" or "a joiner." As such, finding communities—digital or otherwise— might feel less joyful and more chore-ful. As motivation to take this ultra-important plunge, think up one (or several) super-sized incentives to introduce yourself in some creative circles of your choosing. Maybe it's a frozen yogurt feast, or a shopping spree at your favorite independent bookstore. Whatever it'll take to get you out of your comfort zone and into a productive community of like-minded scribes!

Lost and Found

Have you tried all this and more, but you're still struggling to find a foothold in your story? Have you tried stomping your feet and yelling the most ridiculous non–curse words you can think of at the top of your lungs? Have you smudged your workspace with burning sage? Performed an exorcism over your laptop? Oh, writer, I am not making fun, just trying to lighten the mood. I've done all these things and more in dark moments of my own. Blocks that feel this big and deep are exhausting, devastating, and destructive. They erode our motivation and make us forget why we wanted to work on this project in the first place. So, in all seriousness, I do encourage you to shake it off. Don't create a narrative around this temporary hold-up, making it more than it is. It's temporary, eminently fixable, and a blip on the memoir-writing radar—you hear me? After you've thrown your soul-cleansing hissy fit, thrown a shoe, listened to some soothing yacht rock, and you're ready to redouble your efforts, try one, some, or all of these approaches (which I've also tried and actually *do* help).

Write out of order. Who says you have to write your memoir from start to finish? Try writing it from finish to start, or you could lead with some middle bits. Organize your memoir into a list of scenes ranked from things you're most excited to tackle down to those you can't be bothered with right now. As soon as you get stuck, move to the next moment or memory on your list.

_____ _____
_____ _____
_____ _____
_____ _____
_____ _____
_____ _____
_____ _____
_____ _____
_____ _____
_____ _____

Step away from the screen. Don't make yourself sit at the screen if you start to go to the bad place. You don't want to associate writing with negative emotions. Take a break, stretch, breathe deep, and only come back when you've reset yourself again.

Organize (or decorate) your writing area. You know how excited you get about going to bed on fresh-sheets nights? Change the proverbial sheets on your writing area, whether that's a designated desk, a repurposed corner of the dining room table, or any place you can prop your laptop. Make it feel a little fresh and special, as only you know how to do. Declutter, stack your accumulated notes-to-self, and toss those that no longer apply. Add a fun bobble head, some twinkle lights, fresh flowers, a favorite mug filled with freshly sharpened pencils or new pens, or whatever favorite or whimsical accent will reinvigorate the immediate vicinity with good vibes.

Don't keep it a secret. Maybe you don't have a writers' group of any kind, but that doesn't mean you can't talk about your book with nonwriters. When people know what you're working on, they're likely to ask about your progress or mention it the next time you see one another. Having these spontaneous conversations, even—or especially—with people who won't go deep into story structure or literary theory with you, helps you get a fresh and unexpected take on your memoir and may provide the spark you've been seeking.

Be your own advocate. Maybe you already have a cheerleader or coach in your corner, ready with steri-strips and peppy rhymes or a water bottle to refresh you before you go back in for another round of writing. Even if you do have a fan section in the bleachers of life, you know best what encouragement, reassurances, and doubt-slaying words you need most on any given day. Writer, with all the love and care you can summon for yourself, please get in the habit of writing a message (or a couple!) on those Post-it notes you've got on hand. Stick your mini peptalks where you're sure to see them. Swap them out often enough that they remain relevant to the struggle of the moment.

CHAPTER 9

THE RESOURCE ROOM

CHECKLIST

☐ Recommended Reading

☐ More Magical Media

☐ The Can-Do Corner

☐ Food for Thought: What Now?
with Nancy Davis Kho and
Dan Blank

☐ Putting the *You* in Author

☐ Marketing and Publication
Resources

☐ A Fond Farewell

Welcome to The Resource Room! This workbook is filled with challenging activities and exercises, so this space is designed to be relaxing and helpful. Grab a bean bag, put your feet up, and have a glass of cucumber water. Refreshing, right?

While you're chilling out, I'll give you a few quick pointers on what you'll find here when you're ready to hop up and explore the rest of the chapter. Throughout this workbook, you've read the advice and wisdom of over a dozen published memoirists and experts in the genre. You can peruse a list of their memoir and craft titles, all of which make for excellent additions to your Chapter 1 Toolbox. Reading memoirs (and reading about the craft of the genre) is an important and enjoyable way of getting ready to write your own.

To complement this list of books, I have also compiled a list of other recommended media that I've either used or referenced here in *Ready, Set, Memoir!* These are resources I have found invaluable, and feel sure you will, too.

I also find endless encouragement to be crucial to the writing process. You'll find double- and triple doses of "yes!" in The Can-Do Corner, right before you hit the "What now?"–themed resources. There, we've got yet more recommendations for such forward-looking subject matter as your author platform, marketing yourself and your book, and seeking publication.

By the time we say goodbye, you should be armed with all the tools, titles, links, suggestions, and support to exit through the back cover as a memoirist carrying the final draft of a killer manuscript.

But first, finish your spa water and do what you need to do. These resources will be here any time you need them, at any juncture of the writing process.

Recommended Reading

In alphabetical order by author, these titles provide some exemplary fodder for further study of memoirs and how to write them.

- Abigail Thomas's *What Comes Next and How to Like It* (2015), *Safekeeping: Some True Stories from a Life* (2000), *Thinking About Memoir* (2008), and *A Three Dog Life* (2006)

- Andrea J. Buchanan's *The Beginning of Everything: The Year I Lost My Mind and Found Myself* (2018), and *Mother Shock: Loving Every (Other) Minute of It* (2003)

- Brooke Warner's *Write On, Sisters! Voice, Courage, and Finding Your Place at the Table* (2019), and *Breaking Ground on Your Memoir: Craft, Inspiration, and Motivation for Memoir Writers* (with Linda Joy Myers, 2014)

- Daisy Hernandez's *A Cup of Water Under My Bed* (2014)

- Dani Shapiro's *Inheritance: A Memoir of Genealogy, Paternity, and Love* (2019), *Hourglass: Time, Memory, and Marriage* (2017), *Still Writing: The Perils and Pleasures of a Creative Life* (2013), *Devotion* (2010), and *Slow Motion: A True Story* (1998)

- Francesca Lia Block's *The Thorn Necklace: Healing Through Writing and the Creative Process* (2018)

- Kerry Cohen's *Lush* (2018), *Seeing Ezra: A Mother's Story of Autism, Unconditional Love, and the Meaning of Normal* (2012), and *Loose Girl: A Memoir of Promiscuity* (2008)

- Kiese Laymon's *Heavy: An American Memoir* (2018) and *How to Slowly Kill Yourself and Others in America* (2013)

- Leigh Stein's *Land of Enchantment* (2016)

- Meredith May's *The Honey Bus: A Memoir of Loss, Courage, and a Girl Saved by Bees* (2019)

- Mira Jacob's *Good Talk: A Memoir in Conversations* (2019)

- Nancy Davis Kho's *The Thank-You Project: Cultivating Happiness One Letter of Gratitude at a Time* (2019)

- Piper Kerman's *Orange Is the New Black* (2010)

Thanks to these authors for sharing their experiences and advice in these pages. All quotes reprinted here were originally featured on the Write-Minded podcast, listed with my highest recommendation in the next section with other helpful resources.

More Magical Media

For yet more inspiration, check out these resources. In addition to earphones and/or your reading glasses (and maybe some tissues, too, because there is a lot of brilliance and wisdom out there, and it can tug the heartstrings), you'll definitely want to have a pen and paper at hand for the many revelations you're likely to have.

Write-Minded Podcast: Available as a subscription from Apple Podcasts, Google Play, and Stitcher Radio or to stream at podcast.shewrites.com, Write-Minded is a powerhouse of thought-provoking content thanks to its consistently amazing guests (Kwame Alexander, Jeannette Walls, and Carolina de Robertis, to name a few) and thoughtful, accomplished hosts Grant Faulkner of NaNoWriMo and Brooke Warner of She Writes Press.

NaNoWriMo Pep Talks: You won't believe the star power at Nanowrimo.org/pep-talks, an archive of published authors' motivational essays for participants of National Novel Writing Month. Note, especially, such memoirists and writing gurus as Roxane Gay (*Hunger*), Dave Eggers (*A Heartbreaking Work of Staggering Genius*), Anne Lamott (*Bird by Bird*), and Lynda Barry (*What It Is*) among their ranks. I encourage you to read them all, though, for a turbo-charged dose of writerly insight and inspiration.

Pep Talks for Writers: 52 Insights and Actions to Boost Your Creative Mojo by Grant Faulkner: Whether you read these as needed, save one for each week of the year, or read it cover to cover in one or a few sittings, this book is a multivitamin for your creative health. No matter what ails your writing practice, you'll likely find the antidote here.

Julian Friedmann's TedxEaling Talk, "The Mystery of Storytelling": You can watch this agent's take on why great storytelling—and, subsequently, publishing—is so difficult on YouTube at Youtu.be/al3-Kl4BDUQ. He has some controversial ideas, and his advice is not exclusive to written stories (he cites plays and films as well). Whether you agree with him or not, you'll be able to apply many of these concepts to nonfiction writing, giving you plenty to consider regarding your memoir. You probably won't need tissues, but you might laugh.

What other resources do you have in your arsenal when you need creative counsel? Write them here for a complete and personalized go-to list of fail-proof inspiration.

The Can-Do Corner

Mark Your Milestones!

You can cut these pennants out, affix them to a toothpick, and adorn a cupcake or anything really (cheese cube?) as you knock down each writing goal.

Table Tag

Just in case anyone is wondering, make it abundantly clear what you're working on.

I'M WRITING A MEMOIR

You Earned It

You really did. I'm proud of you.

It's Your Party

Draw (or write about) your dream book-release party. Go big! Where is it? Who's on the guest list? What are you eating and drinking? Is there a confetti canon?

Food for Thought: What Now?

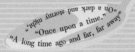

"On a dark and stormy night."
"Once upon a time."
"A long time ago and far, far away."

You've come to end of this memoir-writing workbook, and you've likely got a completed memoir to show for it. You are a star. "What do I do with this memoir?" you may be wondering. Well, you have some decisions to make. Do you want to pursue self-publication or seek traditional publication? Perhaps you're interested in hybrid publishing, which is becoming increasingly popular.

No matter which path you choose for your memoir, you'll need to spend some time thinking about your author platform and marketing strategy. It's a cussed reality, but books don't sell themselves, and it helps if you have a means of advertising your work to a broader audience. To that end, here is yet another (and the final!) Food for Thought.

"Both [my] blog and the podcast were important because I could point to audiences who were familiar with my voice and are likely to buy the book. I'm not saying everyone needs to have a blog and a podcast, but whatever it is— your Instagram feed or your Pinterest page or whatever you do that gives people a consistent sense of who you are and what you're about— you can tie that into whatever creative work you're bringing out into the world."

—Nancy Davis Kho, *The Thank-You Project: Cultivating Happiness One Letter of Gratitude at a Time*

"The way I've always defined author platform is it's about two things: communication and trust. It's about your ability to communicate what you write, why you write it, what you care about. In the process, you're engendering a sense of a trusting relationship—a trusting connection with people. And if you have those two things, you have all of what branding is; all of the platform, all of how to use Twitter, all of what does a book launch and a marketing campaign look like."

—Dan Blank, author of *Be the Gateway: A Practical Guide to Sharing Your Creative Work and Engaging an Audience*

Putting the *You* in Author

Based on Nancy's Food for Thought, think about what online presence you already maintain and could leverage toward an author platform. Publishers will definitely ask, and it will certainly come to bear on your appeal and your book's marketability, so it's better to face this head on.

Do you already have a blog? How is your Instagram following? Alternatively, if you have zero online presence, is there a form of social media you're interested in exploring or feel like you could excel at? Take some time to assess the strength of your social media prowess and plan for how you could either establish or grow your audience.

In his Food for Thought, Dan highlights the importance of "communicating what you write, why you write it, and what you care about" as a means of establishing what he calls "a trusting connection with people." Take a stab at answering these questions and see what you come up with.

What do you write?

_____

_____

_____

Why do you write about that?

_____

_____

_____

What do you care about?

_____

_____

_____

I'm sorry. I promised you this chapter was all fun, all the time, and those last two activities were hard. I tried to do both and decided we should all reward ourselves by coloring in this Mandala.

Marketing and Publication Resources

WeGrowMedia and *Be the Gateway: A Practical Guide to Sharing Your Creative Work and Engaging an Audience:* Don't let Dan's Food for Thought be his only advice to you! Check out his website at wegrowmedia.com, as well as his book, for more of his expert guidance.

Brooke Warner's *Green-Light Your Book: How Writers Can Succeed in the New Era of Publishing* (2016) and *How To Sell Your Memoir: 12 Steps to a Perfect Book Proposal* (2013): Benefit from Brooke's prodigious experience and industry expertise with these resource-rich titles. From her experience as an acquiring, and then executive, editor to cofounding She Writes Press, coaching writers, and having her own work published, Brooke knows the industry inside out.

Writer's Market: *Writer's Digest* publishes this resource annually—usually in the summer—featuring the most up-to-date information for anyone interested in selling their written work. If you're waiting for the newest edition to come out, try to get your hands on a recent copy in the meantime to get an idea of the comprehensive resources it offers.

The Book Doctors (and their book): Visit thebookdoctors.com to learn more about Arielle Eckstut and David Henry Sterry's time- and author-tested services and their industry-approved book *The Essential Guide to Getting Your Book Published* (updated in 2015). These long-time friends of NaNo know their stuff, and they're fun (and funny) to boot.

Swenson Book Development: In addition to sharing her expertise with you in Chapter 2, Jill Swenson is a frequent attendee at her local NaNoWriMo chapter's TGIO (Thank God It's Over) parties. If you haven't been lucky enough to hear her speak in person, you can still gain the benefit of her wisdom at www.swensonbookdevelopment.com.

A Fond Farewell

We have covered a lot of ground together, writer. I can hardly believe the time has come to usher you through the back cover of this book and out into the great beyond. You did magnificent work, and I can hardly wait to hear about your book's journey onto bookshelves everywhere. Will you please give me a shout when it's available, so I can read it?

No matter what happens over the next few months and years, never stop being proud of yourself for doing this hard, courageous, creative thing. You did it! I'll miss helping you along. Come on back if you ever want to give it another go. (I bet next time you'll go through half as many Post-its and finish your timelines twice as fast.) Until that time comes, though, good luck and be well, memoirist. The pleasure has been all mine.

Exit this way, memoirist!

Acknowledgments

Enormous thanks to Grant Faulkner and Brooke Warner for your generosity in sharing the brilliant content of Write-Minded, and to the whole NaNoWriMo family for your time and willingness to make this workbook possible. Warmest gratitude to all the memoirists and experts that shared your wisdom here: Abigail Thomas, Andi Buchanan, Dan Blank, Daisy Hernandez, Dani Shapiro, Francesca Lia Block, Jill Swenson, Kerry Cohen, Kiese Laymon, Leigh Stein, Meredith May, Mira Jacob, Nancy Davis Kho, and Piper Kerman. To Chris Baty and Tavia Stewart, the team behind *Ready, Set, Novel!* and my old-school colleagues, I hope this sequel does the original proud. Thank you for your blessing in writing a follow-up, and for hiring me to be your third musketeer a long, long time ago. I am also thankful to have collaborated on this project with Steve Mockus at Chronicle Books and Lindsay Edgecombe at LGR Literary. We did this during trying times, and you were a dream to work with. And finally, to Pat, my love, I give the lion's share of my appreciation and admiration. Completing this book with a newborn and a preschooler at home full-time in the midst of a pandemic would have been impossible without your flexibility, humor, patience, belief, and impressive domestic capabilities. Thank you.

About the Author

Lindsey Grant is the former program director for National Novel Writing Month. She co-authored the writer's workbook *Ready, Set, Novel!* and is the author of the memoir *Sleeps with Dogs: Tales of a Pet Nanny at the End of Her Leash.*